# THE
# EDGEFIELDERS

Third edition
Copyright 2013 by Judith Wright Favor

Published in the United States by CreateSpace Publishing.
All rights reserved.

ISBN 978-1481224901
ISBN 1481224905
Library of Congress Control Number: 2013901555
CreateSpace Independent Publishing Platform
North Charleston, South Carolina

# What people are saying about The Edgefielders ...

*"Sitting on the porch in the spring of 1936, Margaret Mary notices she feels free. Simply free, like seeing the sun after a wild winter storm."* Such a sense of "freedom" in a "poor house" strikes me as an oxymoron. Can one be really be free under such dire conditions? This story is poignant, yet realistic. It takes sturdy yet delicate writing to capture the challenges of making new friends in old age while wondering about one's absent family. This author does a wonderful job describing both!
    Joanne Hummel, Local elementary teacher
    Observer of the Edgefield Poor Farm for 40+ years

This book will be especially compelling for those who know the importance of shedding light on family secrets, for readers interested in Oregon history and for those who are drawn to Edgefield.
    Dale Stitt, co-founder/director.
    *Journey Into Freedom*

*"When I listen, my whole life becomes the voice of God,"* says Nurse Rachel. Judith composed these stories by listening to her great-grandmother and inmates as they knitted new lives from tangled ends. Margaret Mary's healing begins when a physician honors her goodness and godliness by first sitting with her in stillness, then querying her into self-understanding, strength, and forgiveness.
    Charleen Krueger, Registered Nurse, Knitter

# What more people are saying...

The author depicts a beautiful, practical vision of collective healing energy. Margaret Mary found strength and gift for weaving community through the care of wise, kind healers, inner visitations from magi, inner dialogues, consultation with new friends and old-fashioned Catholic prayers. The Edgefielders learn to abide with pain through creative presence, stories, challenges, singing, harmonizing, moaning, laughing, harmonica playing, ritual and purring. I'll bet the gathering at the end will elicit from many readers, "That's how I want to die!"
    Penelope Mann, UCC Minister; InterPlayer

I see these tales akin to Ignatian contemplation, an imaginative entry into life at the Poor Farm. Those were hard times but these are not hard people. *The Edgefielders* show lovely generosity and a communal commitment to not let hardship beat them down. This book leaves me with hope, and a sense of triumph.
    Frank Rogers, Professor of Spiritual Formation,
    Claremont School of Theology

Care and conversation between Judith and Margaret Mary flow across decades and continue today. The author gives voice to Great Grandmother's journey through the raw edges of mental and physical exhaustion at the Poor Farm as well as the healing that came through the friendships she forged with medical staff and inmates. <u>The Edgefielders</u> helps us become more aware of our ancestors' love, which crosses the threshold of time.
    Jacqueline Chase, Grandmother

# And more.....

Within a decade or two the Great Depression will no longer be a conscious memory in our country. We will know it only through the history books. The personal experiences will disappear, except for novels like <u>The Edgefielders.</u>

This is a rich and earthy tale of those who came before us. The author describes the challenges they faced and how they survived that trying time. This book is reminiscent in time, location, and even style of Denis Johnson's <u>Train Dreams</u>.
  Tim Sunderland, Writer

The characters are very engaging. Vivid descriptions brought them to life; each one has such a gripping story. I can see how this book could be adapted into a screenplay. With more development of the characters, it could make an interesting television series. It probably wouldn't sell on the regular networks but would appeal to a public television audience.
  Judy Leshefka, Meditation Instructor

These stories gave me a chance to vicariously experience living in the Poor House, touching into the hardships, newfound friendships and down-to-earth spirituality of the Edgefielders. This book is a treasure, offering a glimpse into how freedom is discovered in the most unlikely places.
  Barbara P. Anderson, Presbyterian pastor

Who would have known that a progressive government in Oregon created this "poor farm" to provide housing and work for people like Judith Favor's great-grandmother during the Depression after her husband walked out and her children could no longer care for her?

The author paints a vivid picture of friendship, romance, creativity, resilience and the mostly-harmonious blending of religions, races and worldviews in this lovely story of Margaret Mary and the Edgefielders.
　　Claire Gorfinkel, Activist, Writer

This beautifully written book, with fully developed characters, is a personal story of life beyond economic loss. How many of us wonder where today's poor, unemployed people go when they "vanish"?

The wondrous building of relationship between fragile economic survivors described in this book leads me to wonder about today's homeless shelters. Unlike Edgefield, shelter placements - when available today - are usually transient. Thus, in our time, relationships between economically disadvantaged people are sadly transient as well.

In describing a hidden, even shameful, secret about residents at a poor farm from the past, I wonder if the author causes us to reflect on the possibility of the community formed at Edgefield. This possibility of community is mostly absent in our treatment of the homeless today.
　　An incredibly good read.
　　Karen Vance, Kindergarten Master Teacher

# THE EDGEFIELDERS

☙❧

## POOR FARM TALES
*of a*
## GREAT-GRANDMOTHER

Judith Wright Favor

*I have come to believe that by and large the human family holds the same secrets, which are both very telling and very important to tell.*

— **Frederick Buechner, Telling Secrets**

ଓଃ

# Author's Note

A leap of faith led me into composing her story but in the beginning I had no idea what I was getting into. The tales in these pages emerged from my strange and wonderful bond with a foremother who'd become an outcast, a stranger in the family.

By the time I was born in 1940 the hard decisions that put Grandmother Wright in the Poor Farm had become a family secret. By the time I learned of her fate I was old enough to recognize that economic loss may bring spiritual gain. Did this happen for her? I couldn't stop wondering about her experience at Edgefield.

Setting out, I concentrated on connecting with my great-grandmother's reality. Soon I was drawn into the tales of other residents as well. Many good people became involuntary inmates at Edgefield during the Great Depression. Bella's voice, then Ben's filtered into the seams of my imagination. Physical therapist Lily White and Doctor Furst emerged, too, describing the healing contributions of staff. This led me to wonder about religion and spirituality among them. How did people from wildly divergent faith traditions manage to live together during the 1930s? I had more questions than answers. Many were personal.

Could I cast light into the shadows inherited from dearly beloved parents and grandparents who kept my foremother's situation a secret?

Could I reclaim the story of a woman who was treated like an outcast, the one who had become a stranger in the family?

Could I open up more breathing space in the secrecy inherited by coming generations?

*E*<u>*dgefielders: Tales of a Great-Grandmother*</u> is a work of fiction. It sprouted from family seeds that grew in the author's imagination during many seasons. The stories are true although everything may not have happened exactly as depicted on these pages.

My great-grandfather George Albert Wright left his wife in 1933, leaving her destitute. Her son - my grandfather – was out of work with four children to feed. In 1934 Margaret Mary Doig Wright became an inmate at Edgefield, the Multnomah County Poor Farm. I suspect it was shame that caused my ancestors to erase her name from family stories. Fifty years after she died, I came upon her death certificate among some documents. When I asked about my unknown great-grandmother, family members went mute. By then Margaret Mary had been hidden for so long that her descendants could remember very little about her.

Family secrets are both very telling and important to tell. Without them we run the risk of losing track of our true selves. My folks composed an edited version of what happened to Margaret Mary during the Depression. Perhaps they hoped others would find half-truths more acceptable than the full story. Secrets are telling in the sense that they offer glimpses into who we truly are when we're able to look at the full story of who we came from. Why did my aunt close her eyes? Why did my dad shake his head? Why did they close their minds to my curiosity? I sensed that probing into family secrets felt like an invasion of privacy to them.

Margaret Mary welcomed me, though. Her spirit accompanied me as I delved into her hidden past. She encouraged me to dive into the deep places, into the shadows where she had to go before she could construct a new life among paupers. She was my guide into regions where secrets are kept, the dark dangerous ones. Great-grandmother gave me the patience to listen, permission to tell complicated secrets and courage to bring them into the light.

During the Thirties, The Great Depression made headlines. *The Edgefielders* contains few headlines. The tales of the good people of Edgefield are more likely found on the back pages of the newspaper, among the feature stories and the op-ed sections. Obituaries, too, of course. The back pages are the ones I read first.

Nothing tangible remains from the life of Margaret Mary Doig Wright. What became of her thin, worn wedding band? What happened to her trusty old cane? She died before I was born so I never touched her wrinkled cheek. She didn't nestle my head or sniff my downy hair, yet I sense her spirit hovering. No photos remain. No afghan blankets knitted in stripes of wool. No quilts patched together with bits of fabric. No rosary beads. No hairpins. No silver candlesticks. No letters. Only the essence of my great-grandmother endures. I never touched anything of hers, yet we are connected in some mysterious way. The shimmer of her presence raises questions and gives voice to the tales that follow.

My great-grandmother was born on a farm in Hay, Ontario, Canada in 1869. Sixty-nine years later she died at the Multnomah County Poor Farm in Troutdale, Oregon. Only the barest bones of her story are known. Bits came from my dad and aunt who talked around the edges of things, the way we do in our family. The three generations of Wrights in this story are dead now, at rest in the lap of Mother Earth. I'm left to wonder what kinds of stories are buried with them.

During 1939 Margaret Mary's body dissolved in a pine coffin as mine was forming in amniotic fluid. Big things were happening that year. Americans were reading *Grapes of Wrath*, watching "Gone With the Wind" and singing "Somewhere Over the Rainbow." President Roosevelt declared U.S. neutrality in the

European war and the U.S. Department of Agriculture introduced food stamps that year, too late to help my great-grandmother.

Frost touches my temples now. I see my father, long gone, peering back at me from the mirror. The features of the male Wrights show in my face, but I'm discovering that my feelings belong to the females. As I ponder the pain of great-grandparents going their separate ways in 1934, my heart goes with her. I limp into the future with Margaret Mary, following her story with affection and trying to discover how she coped with travail. Sometimes, love has to make hard choices. I take sides with her.

When her husband disappeared in 1934 Margaret Mary worried about him but I don't. I've not been able to connect with George's spirit, with the truth of him, though heaven knows I tried. He only showed his back. I could only imagine his face, a man who kept his eyes on the future – the next scheme, the next diversion, the next romance. The next drink.

Public records show that George Albert Wright died in Portland on October 4, 1944. Aunt Charlotte, Dean's widow, remembers being told that he died on skid row.

Seventy-eight years have passed since George Wright walked out and I am still mad at him for abandoning his wife. She might consider me cold-hearted. So be it. I came by my cold shoulder honestly, inherited from Margaret Mary's own Scottish mother.

# TABLE OF CONTENTS

Author's Note . . . . . . . . . . . . . . . xi
Cast of Characters . . . . . . . . . . . . . xvi
Prologue . . . . . . . . . . . . . . . . . xix

Part One – Margaret Mary: Setting Out, 1934-35 . . . . . 1
Part Two – Margaret Mary: The Journey, 1936-37 . . . . 21
Part Three – Margaret Mary: Coming Home, 1938 . . . 175
Part Four – Edgefield, 1868-2012 . . . . . . . . . 233
Part Five – Judith: Setting Out, 2010 . . . . . . . . 239
Part Six – Judith: The Journey, 1995-2010 . . . . . . 257
Part Seven – Judith: Coming Home, 2012 . . . . . . 263

Epilogue . . . . . . . . . . . . . . . . . 269
Acknowledgements . . . . . . . . . . . . . 275
Questions for Reflection and Discussion . . . . . . 277
About the Author . . . . . . . . . . . . . 283
About the Book . . . . . . . . . . . . . . 283

# Cast Of Characters

**THE FAMILY MEMBERS**

| | |
|---|---|
| Margaret (Mary) Agnes Doig Wright | 1869-1938 |
| George Albert Wright, *husband* | 1868-1944 |
| | |
| Leo James Wright, *son* | 1889-1945 |
| Cordelia Creswell Davis Wright    *Daughter-in-law* | 1890-1961 |
| James Leo Wright, *grandson* | 1915-1998 |
| Margaret Mary Wright, *grand-daughter* | 1917-2006 |
| Virginia Dee Wright, *grand-daughter* | 1927-1969 |
| Dean Robert Wright, *grandson* | 1930-2002 |
| | |
| Albert Wright, *son* | 1892 - ? |
| | |
| James Robert Doig, *brother* | 1873-1944 |

# Cast Of Characters

**THE EDGEFIELDERS***

| | |
|---|---|
| Benjamin Borden* | watch-repairman |
| Bella Monelli* | Italian immigrant |
| Buster Jones* | farm hand |
| Florrie Carter* | housekeeper |
| Fudge aka Mabel May Wood* | friend / knitter |
| Tillie Atkins* | knitter / seamstress |
| Cracker Jack Brown* | disabled veteran |
| Jericho Taylor* | Negro cobbler |
| Lex and Cox* | roughnecks |
| Jasper Carroll* | gay Catholic |
| Joshua Herschel* | Jewish musician |
| Dr. Conrad Furst* | Infirmary Director |
| Dr. Hermann Oppenheim (1858-1917) | Dr. Furst's mentor |
| Dr. Phillip Emmons* | Associate physician |
| Dr. Robert Tait McKenzie (1867-1938) | Lily White's mentor |
| Lily White* | Physiatrist |
| Rachel Cohen* | Jewish nurse |
| Bessie Armstrong* | Negro nurse |

*created from author's imagination

# PROLOGUE

Times were hard in 1935. Comfort wasn't easy to come by. While Margaret Mary struggled with poverty and the threat of homelessness, nearby mills were shut down. Factories along the Columbia River were abandoned. The disaster of the stock market crash sifted down from the mighty to the meek. Bank accounts disappeared. Orders for boots were cancelled. Housekeepers were fired. Sons and daughters had to drop out of school. Roofs fell in and fences fell down.

The Depression damaged many Oregonians. Bella Monelli's overalls and underwear were stolen from the clothesline on the farm where she worked. In Portland, someone broke into Benjamin Borden's jewelry shop and pilfered whatever could be sold for quick cash. Family savings were lost in the bank run and cash was short, so folks traded whatever they had. Jasper Carroll fed his mom and sisters by fishing in Johnson's Creek and bartering speckled trout for a bag of turnips or a clutch of henhouse eggs. As times grew worse in the tailor trade, Joshua Herschel had to exchange a wool vest for an amethyst brooch or a handful of silver teaspoons.

Inmates at Edgefield could hear the low whistle of trains passing through between Hood River and Portland. Some said they carried carloads of orphans who'd been sent out West from cities back East where their parents were starving. The trains didn't stop at Troutdale but stray men sometimes leapt from boxcars when they spied a likely place to stay. Hobos raised shacks from old planks held together by nails collected along the railroad tracks. Passing tramps set fires to keep warm. One bonfire caused serious damage to the Bluegill Tavern near the tracks, where men from the Poor Farm liked to drink. Travelers were on the roads - honest men searching for work and thieves looking for an open window. Folks in Multnomah County began to fear that anything might happen.

Many people did what they could for the lost and forgotten. At Nurse Rachel Cohen's temple, women gathered in the evening to sew and knit for children whose parents were out of work. Nurse Bessie Armstrong went around collecting what little food there was for the needy. Her pastor advised church folks to be cautious with strangers, to lock their doors. Pews at Mabel May Wood's church were full on Sundays, perhaps because the pastor gave out potatoes and apples at the end of every sermon.

Men sat idle on curbs outside shuttered shops, telling big-fish stories and talking about how to get by when there was no work available. Tillie Atkin's pastor preached that faith in God's providence would see them through, but most folks didn't see how they could continue to withstand such hardships. Dogs panted with hunger and hunted rabbits at the edge of town. Feral cats stalked field mice and baby birds.

One rainy afternoon in late January, Ben Borden and Joshua Herschel stepped down from the same trolley and trudged together up the muddy lane. Even though the whole country was crashing down around them, they admitted feeling oddly hopeful out here in the middle of nowhere. Both had heard about men who shot themselves because of their financial woes.

Down-and-outers of all ages, races and religions showed up at Edgefield's Manor House that winter. It was sheer luck that Ben and Joshua could get a bed. They were embarrassed by their circumstances and knew the Poor Farm was the end of the road.

Since everyone was broke, though, they decided to make the best of it. Men who landed at Edgefield sensed they were luckier than some. At least they would have a roof over their heads and enough to eat, though the food was nothing fancy. They'd heard Edgefield was a place where able-bodied men planted the onions, pulled the carrots and milked the cows to feed those who were too frail to do the hard labor. And here, they heard, the women plied their needles, stitched their own clothes and mended for folks who couldn't sew.

Men jostled each other in the chow line, poking fun as Ben and Joshua waited for a meal. Elbow to elbow at long tables, fellows told stories of where they'd traveled, one-upping each other about whose close calls were most dramatic. Soon the two new inmates dug into to what Cook called red flannel hash, potatoes and cabbage fried in lard with a few scraps of beef tossed in. Considering Ben had eaten nothing but hard bread since morning, the hash tasted pretty good.

A bit of income, he told Joshua, might be earned in the basement where Ben had heard craftsmen were encouraged. Redemption, he said, might come to those who worked, and he had skills as a watch-repairman. Ben announced that he intended to ply his trade as soon as he could meet the Director and find a place to set up his workbench.

PART ONE

# MARGARET MARY

☙❦

## SETTING OUT

*1934 - 35*

# ONE

☙❦☙

I wasn't there, of course, but my imagination takes me to the December morning in 1934 when he walked out. If he loved her, how could he leave her the way he did? Love is a complex mix of desires, is it not? I wasn't there when George left the bedroom, calling "Don't wait up," in his self-important way, slinging his suit jacket over one shoulder and striding toward the door. I didn't hear Margaret Mary call, "Bye, George," as she pulled up her stockings. She wouldn't have known this was the last time she'd hear his voice, couldn't have guessed these mundane words were the last they'd ever speak to each other.

As the door slammed behind him she heard the empty canary cage jangle on its metal spring. The Margaret Mary I've come to know in my imagination lifted her chin and tilted her ear toward the cage, listening for Bitsy's sweet song. The canary had cheered her for more than two years, through George's sour silences and unexplained absences. She smiled, remembering how surprised she'd been when her husband knelt on bended knee and presented the canary to her with a courtly bow. Her smile faded as she recalled waking to a silent house last week. She'd found the bird on its back, tiny feet in the air, yellow feathers limp against the stained newspaper at the bottom of the cage. George had buried her bird - her friend - in the flowerbed. She remembered Bitsy's morning concerts and missed the bird's bright spirit. Margaret Mary was the type who became deeply attached to those she loved.

George, now, he was still something of a mystery to her. After forty-six years of marriage, she had grown accustomed to the man's odd ways. There were worrisome things about him. Nighttime knocks on the door, times he stepped out to talk with men she didn't recognize. Some nights he didn't come home at all. Truth be told, she did not want to know why he spent so many nights away. Or, rather, she did not wish to be told. Nor did she want to know what put him in bad moods. Nothing good will come of asking, she said to herself.

There were also endearing things about George, like the gold cross he had given her one Christmas. He'd secured the thin gold chain around her neck so gently, fastened the clasp with such tenderness, that just thinking about it made tears well up. She touched the tiny cross, remembering how generous he could be when he was making good money in the building trade, and how tight things had been since he'd lost his job. Lathe-and-plaster labor was hard on a man his age, but being out of work didn't seem to worry her husband like it worried her. He was one of those free and easy men who slid through life without a care whereas it took great effort for her to manage food, laundry and household accounts. George is lucky, she thought, he doesn't worry about the things that turn my hair gray.

She glanced at his photograph on the dresser, framed in gold. He was a handsome man. Isn't that just like George, she thought, to look so proud and confident in his dark suit and white shirt. He still had a full head of hair – white now - lifting off his forehead in a fine pompadour. He arranged his face to give the impression that George Albert Wright had either just finished smiling or was about to start. His eyes were flirtatious, conveying an intimacy that irritated her to the hilt. Her husband treated every woman with irrepressible charm, even the nuns.

She huffed whenever she heard George tell people he was a Catholic. How could he say such a thing when he hadn't been to Mass for years and never to confession? And to think that he'd acted so religious when they first met. In church of all places. She shook her head with familiar annoyance, shaking loose two hairpins from the bun that kept her thin gray hair in place. Her faded cotton housedress felt too tight around the middle. She loosened the belt and dropped her ample body into an overstuffed chair. I'm getting too heavy, she thought, not for the first time.

Her husband drank, like most men. She figured he'd come home when his gin money was gone.

She puttered around the house. Fretting made her hungry. She munched her way through two days, then five. She practiced how to greet him when he finally came home. How would he act? What would she say? She clutched the gold cross on its chain at her throat, aching with love and fury. George's absence left her confused and embarrassed.

On the sixth day, she stood before the bathroom mirror. George had stood on this very spot admiring himself in the mirror while telling her some tale or another. His pride in himself embarrassed her, though she couldn't understand why she blushed when he preened. Now his disappearance embarrassed her. She wiped a damp washcloth across her face, trying to rub away the flush. The friction only made her skin pinker. She concentrated on composing her features.

What is the suitable expression for a cast-off wife? She settled on stern and resolute.

+++

Margaret Mary held the bag of potatoes and onions in one hand and balanced the butcher's parcel under her arm as she limped up the steps and opened the back door. She felt satisfied, having wheedled the butcher out of a ham hock to season the lima beans just the way her husband liked them. Maybe the smell of beans and ham would bring him back.

As she stepped into the kitchen she lifted her nose and sniffed. Old Spice. George was home. "Helloooo," she called, tilting her voice up into what she hoped was a forgiving tone. No reply. But he'd left a note. She hardly noticed the familiar hurt in her hip as she hurried across the kitchen. She was fixed on seeing what was written on that slip of paper propped against a crusty cereal bowl.

"Don't come looking for me," it said. That's all.

She shook her head and blinked twice, not believing her sixty-five-year-old eyes. But there it was in his loopy scrawl. Five words on the back of a bank letter. George hadn't even signed his name. She turned the page over.

*Foreclosure Notice.*

Her hands shook as she put down the note.

"Don't come looking for me."

The shock of it made her mind go numb. Margaret Mary's legs went weak, too. She almost stepped on the dog, then caught the edge of the table and dropped unsteadily into a wooden chair. That was close. Penny got in the way sometimes, but she was such a comfort to have around.

The Wrights had not wanted a dog, couldn't afford to feed another creature, but the little copper-colored stray kept turning up at the back door. "Like a bad penny," George had said, so that's what they named her.

Today the butcher had slipped an extra beef bone into the packet. Margaret Mary unwrapped the gift and handed it down to the cocker spaniel. She had her own problems to gnaw on. Her husband had come and gone while she was out marketing. He must have been watching the house.

What is that man up to?

Did he come to collect his clothes and shaving gear?

PART ONE : MARGARET MARY SETTING OUT | 1934 - 35

She was too shaky to get up and check the closet, but the idea felt right. Wasn't that just like him to sneak into the house while she was out?

She stared at her husband's scrawl.

Is he coming back, or gone for good?

Her mind whirled.

The mortgage was overdue. How in the world could she ever pay it?

These were hard times. Radio newsmen called it The Great Depression. People were barely scratching by.

Did *Foreclosure Notice* mean the bankers could take her house? She shuddered but couldn't think what to do about it.

Her gaze landed on the cast iron skillet atop the gas ring. The skillet had been a Christmas gift from her aunt many years ago. The sight of it made her mad. She'd grilled countless sandwiches for George. Now she imagined picking it up and smacking him in the back of the skull. *That man melted my good sense faster than a Velveeta sandwich over high flame. Now he's treating me like burnt toast.* The idea made her furious.

*Who do you think you are, talking like that!* George's voice scolded from inside her head.

Oh, dear, this would never do.

She looked at a picture of Virgin and Child hanging above the sink. No help there.

Her eyes went dark with confusion and anger. No matter how hard she focused, the elderly wife could not see into the future, could not see how to get out of her predicament.

After a while she brushed her hair back, lifted the dog into her lap and stroked her silky ears. "There's a lot I don't know, but I do know one thing, Penny. I will never give you up, no matter how desperate things get."

The dog's bright cinnamon eyes met her cloudy ones. Penny's tail thumped sympathetically.

# TWO

☙❧

"**M**other warned me not to marry George Wright. She'd say to me 'There's something about that man that I just do not trust.'"

Since her husband had taken off Margaret Mary had started talking to the dog. Not that George had ever listened much. She threaded a needle and went to work mending an apron, spilling her troubles to the spaniel. "I'd say, Oh, Mother, can't you see how much George loves me and how much I love him? She and I repeated this argument more times than I care to count, which is why I'm glad she's gone to her heavenly reward. If Mother was sitting here now she'd say 'I told you so' and make that snuffing sound in the back of her nose, like this."

The dog looked up and cocked one ear as if to say 'What a rude noise. But do go on, I'm still listening.'

"Then she would pinch her mouth and turn away. My mother was a chilly woman, Penny. She knew how to give the cold shoulder."

She let out a big sigh. "As much as I hate to admit it, Mother was right about Mr. Wright. But he and I did have quite a romance. Want to hear about it?"

Penny nodded her coppery head.

"It's a good story. It all began on a Sunday morning in the year 1887. That's before you were born," she added, smiling down at the dog. "It was early June, but very warm. That's unusual for Montana. I'm telling you about the weather, Penny, because you don't know how cold it can be in Billings in June. Anyway, I was at Saint Mary's, letting my fingers glide over the beads of my Rosary, when a tall, dark man slid into the pew. He moved closer than was seemly. I felt the heat of him and it made my heart pick up speed."

Penny gave a short woof of encouragement.

"The priest, I've forgotten his name - something Irish - droned on in Latin. The handsome stranger kept casting his gaze on me. I was so embarrassed. I bowed my head and tried to keep my mind on Mass, but I had to keep sneaking glances at him through the veil of my church hat. A window was open and the breeze kept blowing my veil back. That embarrassed me until I realized the breeze was helping to cool my cheeks."

"George's hair was striking, wavy and black, not white like it is now. It was unruly, too, falling over one eye. And those eyes of his fairly sparked with light. Well, Penny, you can tell I was quite smitten by the look of him. What I haven't told anyone but you is how excited I was by the heat of him. The longer he looked at me, the hotter I got."

Margaret Mary quickly rose from the kitchen table, fanning her face with a dishtowel. "Goodness, listen to the way I'm going on."

She picked up the dog, stroked Penny's throat and scratched her chin. Penny looked up with wet, adoring eyes and made soft clicking noises in her throat.

Margaret Mary's face wilted as if she might crumple into tears. She wanted to put her head down on the table and wail but Penny whimpered and that changed her mood.

She put the dog on the floor, rose to her feet and hollered "Where are you George?" She squeezed one hand into a fist and shook it at

PART ONE : MARGARET MARY SETTING OUT | 1934 - 35

the ceiling, "Where the hell are you! And you too, God. While I'm at it, I've got a question for you. Where the hell are you in all this?"

Penny thumped her tail encouragingly.

"Oh, no, I'm getting soft in the head, talking to the Good Lord this way."

She wiped the dishtowel across her pink face and announced "Well, that's enough of that."

Stepping to the sink she grasped the cold water faucet with both hands. "And I don't want to hear another drip out of you," she commanded the faucet. "Not another drop of regret!"

Embarrassed by her outburst, she raised her eyes to the picture of Mother and Child on the wall above the sink. "Mother Mary, I need your help right away. Please talk to your son for me. It's urgent."

Outside it was cold and wet. Inside things were heating up. Anger long denied had finally connected an old woman with an untapped source of strength. And she wasn't done yet. "Damn that man!" she blurted.

Penny glowered, in the way that only cocker spaniels can glower. "Excuse me," she said, nodding toward Penny. "I'm not usually one to say swear words, you know that, but George has left me in a terrible fix. God damn him anyway!"

She shouted it again - with full force - and pounded her fist on the draining board. Penny looked up with one ear cocked, as if to ask 'Should I get out of the way?'

Jutting her chin and stabbing her good heel into the cracked linoleum, Margaret Mary declared "I will say DAMN in my own house if I damn well please!"

Penny was impressed. Margaret Mary could tell.

+++

The next morning she examined her face in the mirror and saw aging skin with a pattern all its own. The creases on her face reminded her of sand wrinkles left on the beach after a high tide. Sand and sea endure all sorts of storms, she realized. So could she. So would she.

She dressed carefully in a tidy dark-striped dress with a long skirt. It fell nearly to her shoe tops, disguising the heaviness of her hips and her unbalanced gait. Her broken hip had not healed well. It still troubled her. She laced her sturdy oxfords, brushed her gray hair and neatly pinned a black felt hat on top of her head. Lastly, she folded the *Foreclosure Notice* and tucked it carefully into her purse.

On the way to the bank, her cane made a grave and persistent tapping sound on the sidewalk. It was almost meditative. Moses came to mind, prompting Margaret Mary to lengthen her backbone. The more she concentrated on standing taller and straighter, the more her cane seemed to lengthen too. *Out of my way, you vipers.* She waved her staff with a new sense of authority. "Out of my path, you frisky dogs. I've got a long way to go." Saying the words out loud helped buck up her courage.

Halfway to her destination she heard bird song and stopped to listen. She leaned on her cane, looking up at sparrows lining the electric wire. She uttered a short prayer into the December sky. "Gracious Lord, I know you take care of the sparrows. Please do the same for me. Thank you. Amen."

George had always handled their banking matters so she'd never been to the Oregon Bank. It was a grand edifice. The oak door was firmly shut. She looked through the gilded lettering on the window and turned away, afraid there was no point in entering. Embarrassment reddened her cheeks. Self-doubt weakened her knees. I've never pretended to be smart, she thought. George is charming and I'm just ordinary, but he's not here to take care of business, now is he. She clutched her purse so tightly the *Foreclosure Notice* made a crinkling sound.

A rising sense of fear - and some kind of love - made her persevere. Margaret Mary sensed Moses by her side. *You have not come all this way to give up now,* insisted the prophet. The assurance of Moses steadied her as she pushed through the door. Half a dozen well-barbered heads came up, dismissing her with a glance. She gazed across the marble lobby and spotted Mortimer J. Klein, President. He had a fountain pen in hand, signing something. He was smartly dressed in a navy suit, starched white shirt and gray-striped tie. A white silk handkerchief flared from the pocket of the President's suit-coat.

Tapping her cane with as much authority as she could muster, she stepped toward the wide walnut desk with its gold-embossed nameplate, stately as an aged prophet.

President Klein offered her a chair, which she gladly accepted. She held her breath as he studied the *Foreclosure Notice.* He moved his eyes to her face. He said nothing. The longer he stared silently at Margaret Mary through his gold-rimmed spectacles, the ruddier she became. She'd always hated her embarrassing tendency to blush but now it was agonizing.

"I'm sorry." His tone was level. "The house your husband purchased in 1922 now belongs to Oregon Bank."

"But he's out of work and..."

He held up a well-manicured hand. "I am sorry, Mrs. Wright. It's the law."

"But..."

President Klein cleared his throat and spoke firmly. "Your eviction notice is final on January 31, 1935. You have more than a month to find somewhere else to live."

+++

It was a melancholy Christmas, not merry at all. 1935 got off to a dreary start with a family conference. She hunched against the wallpaper as Leo, Cordelia and the grandkids tried to figure out what to do. Elbows braced on the dining room table, faces scrunched into furrows, voices were tight with tension.

"She can share our room." Margaret spoke for both granddaughters. She was seventeen and Virginia was seven. The girls exchanged looks and nodded in unison.

"The problem is the stairs to the attic are too steep and narrow," Cordelia reminded everyone. "The girls can manage the stairs but Grandmother can't."

"She can have my bed, then," offered Jim. He was nineteen and slept on the screened porch.

"Much too cold for Grandmother to sleep outdoors during the winter," said Leo.

All this talk felt overwhelming to Margaret Mary. It brought up too many cross currents of feeling. In fact, she preferred not to mention her feelings in the company of others, nor did she enjoy hearing how other people felt. Complicated emotions embarrassed her. She kept things to her self. She preferred it when people thought of her as a sweet little old lady. She did her best to act nice on that terrible New Year's Day. Trouble was, she wanted to scream, stamp her feet and hurl the antique candy dish through the window.

As the family tried to solve her situation, she found her voice becoming tight and thin. Each time she tried to get into the conversation, she was obliged to clear her throat and start again. "Grandmother must have a cold," murmured Jim. After that everyone ignored her attempts to speak.

Leo came up with the best idea, offering to go to Oregon Bank and have a talk with the president. Margaret Mary was proud of her son. He'd been Vice President of a bank, so she felt confident he could change Mr. Klein's mind. True, Leo had been out of work since 1929 when Peninsula Bank was padlocked after the crash but she believed in him. Leo was persuasive. She also had faith in her eldest grandson who had dropped out of school to drive a bread truck. He was the one who'd been supporting the family for the last three years. True, they barely got by on what Jim earned.

PART ONE : MARGARET MARY SETTING OUT | 1934 - 35

At Christmas some church ladies brought turkey and yams, but the six Wrights mostly subsisted on beans and bread. How could they feed another?

+++

She was desolate when she heard what happened during Leo's meeting with President Klein. Her son couldn't save her home but he did convince the banker to extend her eviction until February 20, 1935. That was a small mercy. Mr. Klein also told Leo about the Multnomah County Poor Farm in Troutdale. "It's a grand place in the countryside east of Portland," he'd said. "Edgefield is for folks who are down on their luck. Everyone helps out. Men who are out of work raise the chickens, milk the cows and till the soil to feed the lame folks like your mother. It's a good place. I think you should take her there."

+++

Her caved-in chest heaved as Margaret Mary slumped on the edge of her bed. The heavy stale air but her bedroom smelled of memories. Her keepsakes had absorbed her sorrows. She fingered the beads of her Rosary until they were worn thin, the strand unraveling. The cracked leather cover of her Catholic Missal was limp, dampened by tears.

The tattered envelope tucked between the pages of her Bible was brown around the edges. Whose spidery handwriting was on the enclosed note? What did it say? The slender passkey within it was roughened by age. What did the key open? Not even George knew these secrets. And Margaret Mary wasn't telling.

The room was cold. The coal had run out. She hadn't noticed how icy her bare feet had become. Despair can do that to a person. The electric power was shut off yesterday. She had grown accustomed to the chill, too melancholic to care.

Margaret Mary clenched her hands on the lap of her gray woolen robe. *My hands are getting smaller,* she thought, *shrinking with uselessness.* Her flesh evaporated under the weight of her troubles, old bones collapsing from weariness. Since her husband - the only man she'd ever loved - left without a word of explanation, she'd been sinking beneath waves of hopelessness. Now that she was being evicted from the only home she'd ever loved, the old woman was disappearing into shadows of helplessness.

*I'm finished,* she thought, *with all that has kept me alive within these walls.* Skills she'd once used to manage household and marriage were passing from her. She was waiting to pass away, surrendering to the darkness that had come over her. Death lay like a pall at the edge of her vision. It could be a short wait, or a long one. She didn't know. What she did know was that she could only wait for the heavy hand to fall.

Even her dog's wistful sounds fell on deaf ears. Penny whined occasionally but mostly lay quietly under the bed. The coppery spaniel had given up trying to get attention from her favorite person.

+++

"Whose bright idea was it, anyway, to move my mother on the stormiest day of February?" Leo griped.

"Complaining doesn't help," countered Cordelia.

Leo glared at his wife, finding fault in her round face and even rounder figure. I have never liked the way she braids her hair around the top of her head, he thought. He grunted menacingly. Cordelia noted his sound of disgust and decided to ignore it. *We have work to do here,* she thought. *I will put up with my husband's mood until we can get his mother into a cab and settled at the Poor Farm.*

"I will pack Mother's things. I need your father's old Army trunk."

"Where do I find the damn thing?" he growled.

"In. The. Cellar. Leo."

Each word was crusted with frost.

Cordelia stepped into Margaret Mary's room. Her mother-in-law was sitting on the edge of the bed, blue-veined feet dangling toward the floor. She had not spoken since her family burst through the door. Her head drooped toward her nightgown. Face and fabric had faded to the color of the slush clogging Portland's gutters. Her gown hung unevenly over saggy breasts. Her hands lay in her lap like beached fish. Facial skin dragged. Hair stuck to her scalp.

*Why, I do believe she has grown old overnight,* thought Cordelia. *How did that happen?*

"How are you doing today, Mother?"

"Not so good. I haven't slept for more than an hour or two at a time."

"Have you had something to eat?" asked Cordelia, though she already knew the answer.

"No, I'm not a bit hungry." Her voice was dull.

Cordelia realized her mother-in-law's eating patterns had probably been out of order for months. Since George left. Thorns of anger pricked her cheeks red. As much as Cordelia wanted to make things right for this poor old woman - for everyone - she felt helpless. These past two months had been terrible. The Wright family was stumbling along a tragic trajectory. Nobody knew how to stop it.

"Let's get you dressed and combed," she urged. "You look nice in this dress." Her sunny tone didn't fool either of them.

"Here," Leo grunted, dropping his father's dirty Army trunk into his mother's living room floor. "Whose dumb idea was it for me to wrestle this damn thing up the basement stairs all by myself, anyway?" Leo groaned and rubbed his back. He was plagued with low-back spasms. Why didn't everyone hurt as much as he did?

He glimpsed his mother on the edge of her bed, feet dangling. *She looks so unbecoming,* he thought. *My mother needs a good sprucing up.* Leo was a lot like his father. He liked to look upon beautiful women. It pained him to see how unattractive his mother had become. *Will they fix her up out there at Edgefield?* The idea of a beauty salon at the Poor Farm was so unlikely, it made him erupt into splattery anger. "I can't even provide my mother with a decent haircut, let alone a decent home," he yelped like a trapped lion. Leo smacked the wall with the flat of his hand, flung open the front door and slammed it so hard the impact rattled the windows.

+++

The women folded into dark coats and hurried to the taxi. The restless eyes of neighbors peeked through winter-brown berry vines. Margaret Mary wept into her hands as they pulled away from the curb of her home in North Portland. She did not dare look back, could not bear to see Penny chasing the cab. Her neighbor had taken the pooch. She ached at the loss. *Bless you, Penny,* she prayed. *Be as much of a comfort to Esther as you have been to me.*

They sat unspeaking, eyes cast onto wet streets, faces frozen into the masks of strangers. *It's better that Leo didn't come with us,* she fretted, chewing the inside of one cheek. *He might have let loose with one of his tempers. I couldn't bear that today.* She supposed her daughter-in-law couldn't either.

Her thoughts went back to Penny. As she pictured her dog's puzzled eyes, her own welled up. She rubbed the tears away with hands that had gone icy inside her worn gloves. She massaged the swollen finger joints as she turned her face to the streaky glass.

Rubber tires hissed on wet pavement. Wind tossed the evergreens alongside the road. Cordelia sat rigid, her face furrowed. "We'll see you again, bye and bye," she whispered. Those were the only words her daughter-in-law could manage.

*Bye and bye never comes,* thought Margaret Mary. *I learned that in church. I also learned there are times when its best to hold my tongue.*

The taxi man began to whistle under his breath. What was he whistling? *Thou art lost and gone forever, dreadful sorry, Clementine.* When a squeal from the engine made the driver cock his head to listen, he stopped whistling in mid-tune. *Thanks for small favors,* she thought. *I'm already sorry enough without having to think about Clementine's troubles.*

Noisy silence filled the cab. The cabbie's rosary beads swung from the rear-view mirror. He swerved to avoid a pothole and hit it anyway. "Damn!" he swore, then muttered "Sorry."

*Not nearly as sorry as I am,* she thought. *I am in a far worse fix than you are.*

PART TWO

# MARGARET MARY

☙☜

## THE JOURNEY

*1935 - 37*

# THREE

☙

The Multnomah County Poor Farm came into view as they turned from Halsey Street onto a muddy rutted track. A four-story brick building squatted in the middle of winter-bare fields. "It looks like a castle," she whispered. Cordelia wiped the moisture from her glasses before commenting. "It certainly doesn't look poor." Their eyes took in wide porches under protective roofs that decorated three levels. A bell tower perched high atop the structure, poking into bruised-looking clouds.

The cabbie curved around the wide circular drive and braked to a stop at the base of broad steps. A crowd of men stared at them as the women got out. Margaret Mary nervously smoothed wrinkles from her coat. Stubble-faced men in overalls milled around a stairway leading to the basement of the big building. "Pool hall's off limits to ladies," one called out. "No ladies allowed downstairs," shouted another. "Not ever," yelled a third.

She tilted her head to have a look around. Rain pocked the puddles. Drops of water skidded down the side of her face. Everything smelled slippery. A hoarse-voiced man with a veiny face offered to tote her trunk into the building. She nodded yes. Another raw-looking fellow stepped forward to take the other end. "Thank you," she said, Her voice was shaky.

Uneasy under the appraising gaze of dozens of rough-looking men, she firmed her trembling chin and took Cordelia's arm. With baby steps, she made her careful way up the slick stairs and through the front door of her future.

"We call it the Manor House," announced a man with a florid face. He wore a gray cardigan with frayed trousers belted halfway to his armpits. "The big boss calls it Georgian Revival," he added sarcastically. The women gazed up a stylish staircase at fancy cornices and ceilings decorated with wedding cake trims. "This is too grand to believe!" exclaimed Margaret Mary. "I'm used to a small, cozy house. How will I ever feel at home in this palace?" Cordelia had nothing to say to that.

They waited at the registration counter while a clerk with a ginger-orange mustache assembled government papers. Cordelia filled them out. The papers went into a tan folder with Margaret Mary Wright's name on top. She was told to sign the Poor Farm registry.

The women exchanged hasty embraces as the smell of cooked cabbage drifted around them,. Cordelia turned quickly, walked down the stairs and climbed into the taxi. Margaret Mary stood at the window, waving and waving. Her daughter-in-law must have waved, too. *She isn't the kind of person who doesn't wave back.*

The new resident was directed upstairs to the women's ward. She placed one hand on the shiny walnut bannister and slowly made her way up the broad stairs. A stout matron in a stiff blue-and-white striped apron gestured her through the door. Sixty narrow cots marched the length of the room. *At least there are no bars on the window,* she thought with relief. *No curtains, either. At least I can see a bit of sky.*

Always timid in new situations, she was intimidated by the commotion. The ward was crowded with strangers, chaotic with voices, redolent with odors. *A person should be able to get used to anything,* she reminded herself, *even the smell of sour bodies and dirty undergarments. But I can't bear these musty odors right now.* Exhausted by the rigors of the day, she lay down and covered her nose with a folded arm. The familiar smell of her brown-checked flannel dress was a comfort. She dropped into a stupor of exhaustion. No one roused her for dinner. An orchestra of rusty bedsprings and steam radiators disturbed her through the night. It took a long time for sleep to come.

It took even longer to accept her new identity. When Margaret Mary Doig Wright crossed the threshold of the Manor House and signed the registry, she learned that she had become an inmate.

On February 20, 1935 she discovered that all residents of all Multnomah County public facilities - jail, poor farm and hospital - were considered inmates. It was deeply embarrassing to have to live at the Poor Farm, and even more humiliating to learn she would be an inmate for whatever remained of her life. She couldn't bear the thought.

She had always taken her identity for granted. She had always been someone. A daughter. A sister. A cousin. An aunt. A wife, then a mother. A grandmother. Now, all of a sudden she'd been turned into an inmate.

*How will I ever adjust to this?*
*Who will I become in this place?*
She had no idea.
The future was unfathomable.

# FOUR

☙❧

Worry hounded Margaret Mary from her first hour as an inmate. She kept her worries to herself. George had left her. She could not bear to admit that yes, she was married but no, she had no idea where her husband was. That was the truth of it. She hated being an abandoned wife. She stayed in her cot and retreated into prickly silence.

*Where in the world has that man gone?* Swallowing fear made her throat raw.

*Why did he leave without a decent word?* She fretted about her broken marriage.

*Serves him right if he doesn't have anyone to cook for him.* Irritation furrowed her face.

*Who is keeping him warm now?* Jealousy pounded beneath her ribs.

*Who will look after George if he gets sick?* Soon she got sick herself.

The poverty of the place weighed her down. Before long she was too weak to move. Her husband's battered Army trunk squatted like a silent sentry at the foot of her bed. She didn't open it.

The matron scolded. It did no good.

"She won't get up," Matron complained to the Superintendent.

"The grippe," pronounced Nurse.

"Move her to the medical wing," directed Doctor.
The new inmate was too helpless to protest.
Two men hauled her trunk to the basement.
She had not unpacked a thing.

+++

The east wing of the Manor House was the medical ward. There were only ten beds to a room. It was a relief to go from the smelly chaos of sixty cots in the women's ward to the infirmary's quiet atmosphere. The antiseptic scent of alcohol in the air eased her. So did the clean smell of Fels Naptha on her sheets.

She had lost the will to wash her face, to look in the bathroom mirror, to go outdoors. She had lost something before she'd known its worth. She felt completely bereft.

Once a lusty eater, she clamped her lips when nurses spooned potato gruel toward her mouth. Her skin grew slack. Her face took on the color of cold bacon grease. Fasting seemed to suit her. Margaret Mary grew accustomed to the tart taste of loneliness.

+++

The sea around her never rested. The deep waters never slept. The tears never ceased. The ocean moaned against the beach, tossing eternal waves of sadness against rocky shores. Memories of her son Albert tore at her heart and left tooth marks on her soul. The boy left home when he was eighteen and hadn't been seen since. Memories of her husband sank her into an abyss of sorrow so deep that she feared drowning. She was shipwrecked, a cast-off wife, a failed mother. She moaned, clinging to her bed as if to a life raft. She suffered aches of body, fevers of mind and confusions of spirit. Grief gripped her face. Loss ripped her heart. Darkness clouded her mind. Mourning was an exhausting business.

+++

Another drizzly day. Margaret Mary awakened to a ward gloomily lit. She felt drizzly, too. A morning layer of fog wrapped her in its dismal haze. She'd slept for twelve hours but was still bone tired. Her mind felt drowned, her body heavy as an anchor. Lacking the will to lift herself up, she pulled the covers to her chin. Squalls of depression had blustered through her for weeks, following a predictable weather pattern. Whenever she woke it hovered close, a weighty marine layer dampening the monotony of the day. The fog refused to recede.

+++

"I'm Dr. Conrad Furst, Resident Director of the Infirmary." He introduced himself quietly, courteously. His accent alarmed her. "Where did you come from?" Her voice croaked.

"I emigrated here from Cologne. With my wife." He spoke softly, reassuringly. "We did Quaker resettlement work in Germany after the Great War."

She glanced beneath pale eyelashes at the tall, stooped man. His cheeks gleamed pinkish beneath a stubble of white whiskers. His eyes looked kind.

"I'll be taking care of you with the assistance of Dr. Phillip Emmons" he went on, gesturing toward a freckled young man with big ears.

"How are you feeling today?" Dr. Furst's voice sounded milky to Margaret Mary. It felt like warm, sugary cocoa. The sound of his voice soothed her back to sleep. She didn't respond the next day, either when the two doctors saw her during morning rounds.

Dr. Emmons held her case file. "Says here that she walked in under her own steam," he said. "Husband George lost his job in construction and walked out on her. Eldest son Leo, an unemployed banker with too many mouths to feed, sent her here. Second son Albert, whereabouts unknown. Homeowner. Mortgage payments in arrears. Foreclosed in December. Evicted last week."

The young doctor had an eager look on his face. The Medical Director had selected him for this position from a dozen applicants. Dr. Emmons had just finished medical school at Oregon State and wanted to prove himself worthy of the older man's confidence. He closed the file with a snap. "What's your tentative diagnosis of Mrs. Wright, sir?"

"Physically, she has symptoms of articular rheumatism but its not the rheumatism that concerns me most," said Dr. Furst. He rubbed one palm across his shiny scalp and smoothed the sparse ring of white hair curling around his ears. He gazed down at the patient. Margaret Mary's eyes were open but unfocused. She seemed unaware of them.

"Have you heard of traumatic neurosis, my boy?"

Dr. Emmons shook his head.

"I suspect our patient is suffering from a state of melancholy. As a young doctor, I studied under Dr. Herman Oppenheim in Berlin. I found his views on traumatic neurosis quite convincing."

"Can you teach a new American doctor how to diagnosis that?" asked Dr. Emmons. His observant hazel-green eyes moved back and forth between his tall colleague and the small, prone patient.

"It is characterized by nervous symptoms in the body that begin in the mind," explained Dr. Furst. "Patients with Mrs. Wright's symptoms have usually suffered a severe trauma."

"What sort of trauma?"

"It's too soon to know. And she's not talking. That's why I begin by sitting in silence with the patient."

"Why...?"

"So she knows she's not alone in her suffering."

"How...?"

"Dr. Oppenheim taught that physical reactions to fright may often cause molecular changes in the tissues."

"That's a new idea to me," said Dr. Emmons, shifting from one foot to another, hands jammed deep in the pockets of his lab coat.

"Yes. It may not be well known in this country. Dr. Oppenheim presented case studies at a conference of German neuro-psychiatrists in Munich in 1916. His ideas have been causing controversy among physicians ever since."

"I don't mind controversy. But what leads you to this diagnosis?"

"In Mrs. Wright I sense a connection between melancholy and neurasthenia. Soldiers called this condition shell shock. In Germany, after the Great War, I treated many people burdened by similar symptoms."

"But what good does silence do?"

"Quakers see the possibility of goodness in each and every person. Shared silence can reduce inner turmoil and help patients touch their own goodness. A quiet presence can sometimes bring melancholics back to their senses."

"And how will you treat the rheumatism?"

"It may be soft-tissue rheumatism, which can also cause significant discomfort. We'll treat it with cod liver oil. More importantly, we will watch, listen and ask questions."

# FIVE

☙☙

I'm not sure what Margaret Mary would have thought of Rachel Cohen. The nurse's Jewish name, prominent nose and dusky coloring might have given her pause, had the patient been alert enough to notice. She wasn't.

Rachel came on duty at eleven each night. She wore a starched white uniform, a calm demeanor and a quiet competence. Her ministrations to the elders went far beyond what she'd been taught in nursing school. Yes, Nurse Rachel took temperatures, measured pulses and administered medicines. She also took the spiritual measure of souls entrusted to her care. It suited her to work the night shift where her prayers could circle luminously through the infirmary, landing light as moths upon the brows of sleeping patients.

Margaret Mary was unaware of Rachel's presence as she tossed and turned. Her focus was inward. She spent her troubled nights in distant realms, riding the rails with her missing husband. She wanted George back but if she couldn't have that, then at least she wanted to keep him alive. She had, after all, married 'til death do us part, so she kept praying for her husband, alerting Mother Mary whenever she sensed George was in danger. She devoted what little energy she had to protecting her wayward man from gypsies, hobos and loose women. She would have been surprised to hear that anyone knew of her mission. She was hardly conscious of it herself. But Rachel Cohen was a highly attuned nurse. She sensed some sort of hidden potential in Mrs. Wright and this intrigued her.

Had we been able to listen in on Rachel's inner dialogue, we might have heard her whisper "There's something about this woman that reminds me of Jacob in The Torah. Mrs. Wright seems to be wrestling with a power larger than her self. Could it be the same angel Jacob encountered?" Standing at the foot of the bed, Rachel slipped into a prayer that was as familiar as breath itself. *Sh'ma, Sh'ma, Sh'ma* she whispered as she smoothed the rumpled sheets. *Sh'ma,* "Hear O Israel."

+++

Had the patient been awake and alert, her natural curiosity would have brought out the story. Margaret Mary would have asked how prayer had become the nurse's primary language during her sixteenth summer. She would have listened to Rachel tell of drowning in Blue Lake, how she went under, how her mind went dark. How Chad, her frightened beau, pulled her onto the beach, rolled her onto her stomach and straddled her slender waist. How the gathering crowd held its collective breath as he lifted her shoulders and thumped on her back until the art of artificial respiration made her gag and retch. How she had come back to life sputtering an ancient prayer, spewing *Sh'ma, Sh'ma* until her lungs were clear.

Witnesses described how her face had changed color from lard white to peony pink. She did remember saying *Sh'ma, Sh'ma* as Chad helped her sit, then rise to standing. "You looked dazed, yet radiant," he'd told her later. She did remember drawing fresh air into sore lungs as the crowd found its collective voice. She remembered how strangers on the beach - Christians as well as

Jews - intoned *Sh'ma, Sh'ma, Sh'ma* to celebrate her return to life.

Had they been conversing, Nurse Rachel would have told Margaret Mary she preferred to work graveyard shift so she could pray through the night. The quiet infirmary was her temple, though no one else knew this. My great-grandmother might have squeezed Rachel's hand to show that she understood when the nurse described how the spirit of her grandfather kept her company through the long nights. His companionship strengthened her soul, she said. Margaret Mary would have nodded. The patient longed for that kind of closeness, and dimly recalled the kindly soul of her own long-departed grandfather.

As rapport between them deepened, Rachel might have tried to explain the mystery, how she sometimes sensed the oneness of all things while tending the sick. How, over the course of three decades, *Sh'ma* had worked its way into the marrow of her bones. How this simple prayer had become Rachel's essence, her origin, her life-blood, her very home. How she shared the divine gift of *Sh'ma* with her sleeping charges, though most were not aware of it. How she quietly recited the ancient words of Deuteronomy in Hebrew as she walked the aisles of the infirmary. *Sh'ma Yisrael, Adonai Eloheim, Adonai Ehad.* "Hear, O Israel; Yahweh, our God is the one Yahweh...You shall love Yahweh your God with all your heart, with all your soul, with all your strength..."

# SIX

☙☙

"Humpty dumpty sat on the wall — "
Nurse Bessie heard Mrs. Wright thrashing in her sheets and mumbling in her sleep. Bessie Armstrong moved quickly for a wide-hipped woman. She set down her medicine tray and laid a broad, black hand on the patient's brow which was overheated. Margaret Mary's breath was short and shallow.

Bessie bent close to listen and caught lines from an old nursery rhyme.

"Humpty Dumpty ... fell ... Albert ... cracked."

Nurse Bessie called for Dr. Furst who came right away. "I'm here," he said, in his soothing way.

"Humpty broken, broken ... Dumpty ... can't put back together."

"I'm with you, Mrs. Wright. You may feel as if you're in the valley of the shadow of death, but you're not alone. Something's broken you said."

"Wall ... son ... Albert ... big boy ... bashed the wall ... smashed ..."

"Smashed you? What got broken?"

"Pushed, cracked me." She placed both palms on her upper chest, moaning softly.

"Your son broke your shoulder?" No, the patient shook her head.

"Your clavicle? Your breastbone?" Yes, she nodded, eyes tightly shut.

"I am so sorry, Mrs. Wright. A cracked clavicle is painful. Is it hurting now?"

The patient shook her head.

"Tell me about Humpty Dumpty. Did something else fall and break?"

"Police ... Albert ... pet shop ... animals burned alive ..."

Dr. Furst gazed at her, concern wrinkling his forehead. "Your son set the pet shop on fire?"

A grimace twisted her face. Her eyes were squeezed tight.

The doctor gazed at her with tender concern.

"When a troubled child pushes his parents to the wall, something often breaks," he said.

Yes, she nodded without opening her eyes. "Marriage."

He placed a hand on the back of her wrist and breathed quietly.

"Love, too," she whispered, turning over and burying her face in the blanket.

Dr. Furst rose after a while and touched her shoulder. "I'll be back tomorrow. Nurse Bessie is nearby. You're not alone."

+++

Violent visions splintered her days and nights. Shouts in Italian and German pierced the soundtrack of her nightmares. She heard bottles breaking, men pummeling each other, sirens wailing. She smelled whiskey, urine and crusty overalls. She sensed feet running and knives flashing. She glimpsed throats slashed, heads dangling. Blood pattered onto trampled dirt. She heard limp bodies hit the ground and gypsy women keening in a high-pitched foreign tongue.

+++

PART TWO : MARGARET MARY THE JOURNEY | 1935 - 37

As she fought her way up from sleep one morning, the nightmare stuck to her like pitch. A heavy-breasted woman with runny eyes was pushing her wet mouth against George's ear. She whispered in a flirty voice "Come with me, mister, and I'll change your luck."

"No! NO! Don't go!" She was screaming.

Nurse Bessie was at her bedside.

"Mrs. Wright, wake up. You're having a bad dream.'

"I've got to warn him," she yelled.

"Hush, you're frightening the other patients. Warn who?"

"My husband," she replied.

"Here, let me help you sit up," said the nurse. "You're flushed. Here's a drink of water."

Margaret Mary flung the cup away and looked wildly from side to side.

"No, no!" Her voice rose to a shriek of panic. "George must not go with that woman. She's got syphilis."

+++

She lay wasted and still, like a storm-tossed body on a barren shore.

"I'm here with you, right here," said Dr. Furst. He had come to her bedside every day since the syphilis incident. Sometimes he listened and asked questions. Sometimes he simply rested a hand on her arm and sat quietly beside her. Today he bowed his head and invited the Light.

+++

"Good morning, Mrs. Wright. Today is summer solstice."

"Good, Doctor. I need you."

"What's happening?"

"Trains shrieking. Hobos screaming. There's a leg on the rails spraying blood. Men are watching but nobody is helping. Is it George?"

"I don't know, Mrs. Wright. Do you sense your husband has been injured?"

"I don't know. It was an awful dream."

"Painful dreams may seem like tidal waves but they don't last forever. Does dreaming about your husband make you feel worse?"

"I couldn't feel any worse."

"Experts say that dreams bring up feelings we can't accept when we're awake. Rage. Attraction. Sorrow. Fear. Bad dreams are like bullies. They batter the strength out of you, steal all your energy."

"They do. They have."

"Melancholy is the body's way of saying it's time to face these inner bullies and demons."

"I'm too tired for that."

"It's natural to feel like you're lost at sea but the only way home is through the storm. Hang on and face into the wind. I know it sounds opposite. You want to get away from the tempest but the only way home is to ride out the storm."

"Why? Why do I have to do that?"

"Your body is showing us that something in you wants to prevail over your fears. Your soul wants to get strong."

"I don't like to fight."

"I know. I've been there. And I've been with others who've gone through these sorts of storms. They've all said it's scary as hell."

"It's terrifying. It wears me out."

"I don't know what kind of ghosts you'll see or what demons you'll still have to face, Mrs. Wright. But I'm here."

"Not all the time."

"No, but Nurse Bessie is here during the day and Nurse Rachel at night."

"I don't know how to do what you say I have to do."

"Not yet, but you will. I know one thing, and I'm certain of it. This is your soul's journey. And your soul will show you the way."

+++

"What day is it?"

Dr. Emmons was holding her wrist, taking her pulse. "August 26. Why do you ask?"

"I got married on August 26. I'm remembering the first time I met my husband."

"Where was that?"

"1887 in Billings, Montana. It was a hot day in June. We met in church, at St. Mary's. George sat in my pew."

"Your heart rate just doubled, Mrs. Wright, and your face just became suffused with blood. Want to tell me why?" Dr. Emmons gave her a small, amused smile.

"I was so embarrassed. George was such a handsome man. He kept looking at me during Mass and the breeze kept blowing my veil back from my face. I knew it wasn't seemly but I couldn't help looking at him. His eyes were so bright."

"Hmmm, sounds like the beginnings of a great romance."

"It was, and the end of my becoming a nun. George didn't know I was planning to join the convent. He slid so close I could feel the heat of him. My heart melted right there in the pew. The longer he looked at me, the hotter I got."

"Sounds like mutual attraction to me."

"You would have been impressed with George. He was a dapper man, trousers pressed into sharp creases. Not a speck of dust on his black shoes. How things have changed…"

# SEVEN

☙❧

"Up and at 'em," said a lean, muscular woman with a commanding voice. Alabaster skin shone tight across her cheekbones. Obsidian hair streaked with gray was pulled back from her face, held in place with a silver clip. The new physical therapist wore a slim black skirt and a black open-collared shirt topped with a white lab coat.

Briskly she swept back the covers with one hand and slid the other beneath Margaret Mary's shoulders. "Atta girl," she cheered, reaching an arm under the patient's knees and swiveling her own hips to launch the bedridden woman's feet over the edge of the bed. They hadn't touched the floor for months.

"I'm Lily White, your physiatrist," she said in a clipped British accent.

The patient looked stunned, but interested. "You're who?"

"Lily White. Don't you dare laugh. No clever quips about my name, either. I've heard them all."

Margaret Mary held back a grin. "All right. You're my what?"

"Doctors call me a physiatrist. You can call me Coach. It's my job to get you back on your feet and walking. See this contraption?" She pulled a four-wheeled metal frame into view. "Physical therapy. Doctor's orders."

"I'm too weak to walk."

"That's not what Dr. Furst says. That man worked with wounded German soldiers. He got them up and walking after they'd been shot and bombed. I did the same in England. You're in good hands here."

Lily was all angles, not a bit of fat on her. Not a ghost of a smile, either. She put Margaret Mary in mind of Ebenezer Scrooge. The woman was all business and scowls.

Lily slid a pair of gray felt slippers onto Margaret Mary's puffy white feet, looped a wide canvas belt around her waist and leveraged the startled woman up to standing before she could protest.

"Hang on," she instructed, curling the patient's hands around the handlebars.

"Off we go now." Lily held the belt taut, stood close behind her shaky patient and nudged. One wobbly step became two, then three.

"Isn't this enjoyable now," said Lily. It wasn't a question.

Margaret Mary was trembling too hard to reply.

"About face," commanded Lily, using body English to direct the maneuver.

"I'm tipping," said the patient, flailing one arm, but her coach deftly tugged and blocked the fall with her hip. "There you go, set to rights."

Back at the cot, Lily counter-balanced with her own body and gradually lowered Margaret Mary into bed.

"You'll get yourself in the habit before long," she said reassuringly. "Before you know it, you'll be walking all the way down the hall to the loo."

The patient shook her head, too tuckered to talk.

"None 'a that, now. I'll be back tomorrow, luv."

+++

The next morning, Margaret Mary awakened to the smell of cigarettes and the sensation of someone massaging her feet. It was Lily, rotating her ankles then pressing thumbs into the soles of her feet.

"Ow, ow, OW," she protested.

"None 'a that, now. Don't you be upsetting the other patients with your fuss."

Her breath smelled of tobacco and something else, too. What was it?

Lily's hands pressed into her calves, pushing and pulling on muscles that had lain dormant for months. The coach's palms were surprisingly soft against the patient's skin.

"What is that smell?" Being touched gave Margaret Mary courage to ask an embarrassing question.

"Kools," said Lily. "Menthol mixed with tobacco. I love the taste. Kools are healthier than Bensons and easier to buy in this country. Getting costly, though. The price of a pack has gone up from a dime to fourteen cents."

+++

Margaret Mary began looking forward to her sessions with Lily White, who came almost every day. She never knew what time her coach would show up. What would this new physiatrist do? Comforting massage? Or would Lily insist on challenging exercises to stretch her flabby muscles? Would they take another frightening excursion on her feet? Would she have to push the wheeled walker across the ward? Lily mixed it up. She supposed variety was part of the plan.

+++

During morning rounds on the first of November, Dr. Furst and Dr. Emmons wished her a happy birthday. She woke up hungry for the first time since February and celebrated her sixty-sixth year by eating two bowls of mush. Nurse Bessie helped her to the communal lavatory and into the claw-footed tub. The hot bath felt delicious after months of bed baths. It was a celebratory soak. She tried to brush her own hair, but the effort wore her out. Bessie finished the job. Lily White gave her the day off.

Leo's family arrived just before sunset, bearing gifts. Her son presented three tall yellow chrysanthemums in a milk bottle. Cordelia brought a hand-sewn nightgown of cotton flannel sprigged with yellow and white daisies. Virginia was learning to bake. She had decorated a chocolate cupcake with yellow icing just for Grandmother. Dean, her youngest grandson, crayoned a rising sun on butcher paper, accented with tangled lines of bright red and green.

The family visit lifted her spirits but drained her strength. By the time they departed she was exhausted. She slept for two days.

+++

Lily White awakened her by pressing sensitive spots on the sole of one foot.

"Ouch!" protested the patient. "I never know what to expect with you."

"Good morning to you, too. Why do you have yellow flowers on your bedside table?"

"A gift from my family," she began. Lily cut her off.

"Never have liked yellow," she asserted. "Cowards are yellow."

"Cowards? What do you mean?"

"Liars, thieves, cheaters. People who are not with the plan. I can't stand cowards."

"Not with the plan?"

"Yes. Are you a coward, or are you with the plan?"

"What plan?"

"My plan, for getting you strong."

"Well, I think so...."
"Too weak. You sound cowardly."
"Well, I'm not. Yellow is a sunny color, not a cowardly one."
"So you can chuck it right back at me, then."
"Yellow makes me happy."

A quick grin crossed Lily White's face. It was the first time Margaret Mary had seen her physiatrist smile.

"So, are you in, then? In with Dr. Furst's plan for you to walk again?" Her tone was hearty.

"Yes!" Margaret Mary's was emphatic.

"Good, then. At the end of the day, the plan is to reach an increment of improvement. So, let's get moving."

+++

A few nights later something stirred Margaret Mary into wakefulness. Perhaps it was the mighty wind off the Columbia River shaking the infirmary windows in their frames. Something captured her attention. Maybe it was the mysterious murmuring sound of a language she did not understand. *Sh'ma Yisrael, Adonai Eloheim, Adonai Ehad...*

She perked up both ears and listened. "Let these words be written on your heart... *Sh'ma Yisrael, Adonai Eloheim, Adonai Ehad.*

Something made her shiver under the blankets although s didn't feel cold. Her body and mind seemed to be dissolving. She couldn't stop the odd sensation, nor did she want to. The shivers came from beyond herself, something like awe. She felt a kind of oneness, a sense of unity with everyone and everything. The experience was strange and wonderful. She let herself go, surrendering into a vast ocean of love.

*Sh'ma, Sh'ma, Sh'ma ...*

# EIGHT

႗႘

By Thanksgiving she was beginning to take an interest in the activities going on around her. *So this is what it's like to return to the land of the living.* She pulled herself up, leaned against the headboard, and watched the nurses tending to the other nine patients.

Would her family come today? She hoped not. She wasn't up to chatting with a crowd of visitors.

Nurse Bessie's teeth gleamed against her walnut skin as she grinned, handing her a tray. Bessie always smiled. "You've got to eat if you want to be discharged from the sick ward." Margaret Mary's appetite still wasn't good. Pale turkey, lumpy spuds and canned peas didn't smell appetizing. She glanced at Edna, groaning in the next bed. *At least I'm not suffering with the cancer.*

What a depressing way to spend Thanksgiving, picking at such forlorn food. She wanted her husband to take her home. She wanted to smell Cordelia's oven-browned turkey. She wanted to see Leo standing at the head of the table with a silver carving knife in one hand and a scroll-handled silver fork in the other. *The carving set we got for our wedding, the set George and I received in 1868 and passed on when Leo and Cordelia were wed in 1913.*

In her mind's eye, she pictured George as he'd looked on their wedding day. She imagined him riding a white stallion into the

Infirmary, scooping her up and galloping off. She imagined tucking her nightgown between her thighs, wrapping her arms around her husband's waist, burying her face in his neck and cantering into the future together. She wanted to start over. But no matter what she wanted - no matter how hard she hoped for rescue - she recognized that her yearnings had no influence on her husband. No influence whatsoever. *He is lost and gone forever. Dreadful sorry, Margaret Mary.*

She wasn't ready to give up the security of the infirmary but she was getting weary of being dull and listless. In lucid moments - like this one - she realized George would not be coming for her. Not today, not on any Thanksgiving. *I have no idea what he is up to.*

*Whatever I learn about him,* she declared to herself, *I will say Oh. I should have known.* Whatever George is doing, she decided, it would have a familiar quality. *Of course. That.*

+++

Lily White appeared, ashtray in one hand, a glowing Kool in the other, straps of a gingham bag looped over one arm. "A happy Thanksgiving to you," she said with a small half smile. Her voice had a mocking tone.

"What're you doing here? I thought holidays meant a break from therapy."

Lily stubbed out the cigarette and set the ashtray on the bedside table. "It's just a Yank holiday, you know. We Brits don't idolize turkeys."

"It's about thanking, not idolizing..."

Lily cut her off. It was a habit of hers. "Do you know how to knit?"

"Knit. Yes, I learned when I was a girl but..."

"Well, then, here's something to cheer you up."

She upturned the red-checked gingham bag onto Margaret Mary's lap. Out tumbled an enormous tangled mess of yarn. "Beige, brown or yellow?" asked Lily. "I know, you'll want yellow," she interrupted. "The cowardly color."

Margaret Mary shook her head. "You know better," she said. She'd grown to enjoy being teased by Lily.

"Ready for your first lesson in physiotherapy? This tangle of yarn illustrates on the outside what your muscle spindles look like on the inside."

"Spindles? I'm not following you, Lily."

"The reason you're having such a hard time getting your legs working again is that you've got muscle spindles. Ever seen a snag in a sweater?"

"Well, yes..."

"Ever snagged it yourself? Caught your sweater on something and pulled the yarn?"

"Yes." Margaret Mary's face puckered, like a child trying to figure out a problem in math.

"So, the tangle in your lap illustrates the trouble at the core of your leg muscles. Spindles are like snags. They reduce the supply of oxygen and nutrients into the trigger points. Your muscles don't have enough energy to pump calcium outside your cells where it belongs. Your job is to sort out this mess and roll each color into its own ball."

"What does untangling yarn have to do with my leg muscles?"

"It's therapy. Meant to loosen up the affected muscles so they can relax."

"I don't see the connection."

"Don't trouble your mind about it. I made the connection. One of us is enough."

+++

As her fingers worked the yarn free of knots, Margaret Mary grumbled to herself, continuing the discussion with Lily in her mind. When Nurse Bessie stopped to visit, she tried to explain why she was doing this, but gave up after two awkward starts. Bessie nodded as if she understood anyway and went about her work, humming.

"What's that you're humming?"

*There Is A Balm in Gilead.* It's the anthem my choir will be singing next Sunday. I do love the Grace Gospel Choir, yes'm, I do." Margaret Mary saw a shine in her pecan-brown eyes.

Next day, Lily arrived with two shiny knitting needles poked crossways in her dark hair, just above the silver clip. She posed like a starlet, turning this way and that so Margaret Mary could get the full effect.

"Very fetching," said the patient.

"Thought you'd like my new look," said the physiatrist. "Here, they're for you," she added, drawing the needles out of her hairdo with the flourish of a sword-fighter.

"No walking for you today," she announced after a diagnostic massage of the patient's calves and thighs. "Too many tight muscle spindles."

"Look," said Margaret Mary, holding up three fat balls of yarn. "I got all the tangles out." She sounded like a schoolgirl presenting her artwork to a critical teacher.

"Well done," announced Lily, playing her part as the schoolmarm. "Very neatly wound. Now for your next task. Would you rather knit a lap robe for Mr. McCarthy or baby booties for the newest resident of the Medical Corps?"

"I'm rather out of practice at knitting," Margaret Mary mused. "A flat lap robe is simpler. Why does Mr. McCarthy need one?"

"He's a cold-blooded Scot with the tremors. Says his shins are always a'shiverin'."

"And whose baby needs booties?"

"Dr. Emmons and his good wife Priscilla just had their first child, a girl. She's been keeping everyone awake in the medical quarters. I live upstairs with the nurses, above the doctors' units. That tiny tot has a mighty voice."

"Maybe she's crying because she has cold feet. I'll save the buttery yarn to make booties for her, but first I'll practice on Mr. McCarthy's brown and tan afghan."

+++

"How'd you come to know about muscle spindles, anyway?" asked Margaret Mary a few days later. She'd been puzzling over Lily's lesson as her hands were busy knitting.

"I studied neuromuscular techniques in Europe," Lily replied, "or NMT as it's known in England. I served under Dr. Robert Tait McKenzie. We developed corrective exercises to treat men who'd been wounded in the Great War."

"How'd you get to Oregon?"

"They sent me across the pond to study in Canada, then on to teach courses in physiotherapy at Reed College. McKenzie's text *Reclaiming the Maimed* was what I used to train women to treat men with war wounds."

"So there are other women like you?"

"Yes, quite a few of us. We formed a chapter of the National American Women's Physical Therapeutic Association in Portland."

"What did people call you?"

"Reconstruction aides."

"Well, you're certainly reconstructing me," grinned the patient. "I do believe I'm ready to start knitting yellow booties for the baby next door."

# NINE

☙❧

"**M**erry Christmas, Mrs. Wright! Glad to see you sitting up in an armchair."

"What are you doing here, Dr. Furst? This is a holiday."

"I volunteered to make Christmas rounds so Dr. Emmons could celebrate with his family. Did you know they named their new baby Mary?"

"Are they Catholic?"

"No. Presbyterian."

"Well, they couldn't have picked a finer name," she replied. "Glad they didn't saddle her with Agnes like my mother did."

"How did Mary become your middle name, then?"

"Long story, doctor."

"I've got all day. Our patient load is the lowest it's been in two years. There's nothing I'd rather do this Christmas morning than hear a Mary story."

She gazed over his head and turned her face toward the northeast as if looking toward her origins. "I wasn't laid in a manger," she grinned, "just a wooden cradle in a bare farmhouse in the village of Hay. Rural Ontario."

He dipped his head as if acknowledging the humor of coming from a place called Hay.

"Mother named me Margaret Agnes Doig. George added the Wright."

Memories of childhood formed and dissolved in her mind. "I had to run fast to get away from the ragged boys throwing stones at me. The rocks were easier to dodge than the nickname. They chanted Maggot, Maggot, Maggot Face and I hated being called Maggot. It made me feel so ugly. So ashamed."

She paused to wipe her face with the sleeve of her cotton-flannel nightgown. The daisy-sprigged fabric absorbed some of her heat. Dr. Furst sat quietly, nodding as if he understood how such boyish behavior could cause a young girl such anguish. *He's so calm,* she thought. *I like that in a man.*

"I hated Maggie Aggie, too," she went on. The other nickname, the one the girls called me. I told them my true name was Margaret Agnes and I didn't like Maggie Aggie but they called me that anyway."

"When did you change it to Mary?"

"In the convent."

It felt risky to tell this part. She glanced at Dr. Furst. His face shone with kindness. She felt safe to go on.

"I started out to do holy work," she said in a low voice. "I left home with Sister Katherine, to become a nun, to start a new convent in Montana. That was the only way Mother would let me leave Hay. And I really did mean to complete my novitiate," she said in an insistent voice. "I did, honest."

Dr. Furst's pale blue eyes gleamed at her. She sensed his care, but suddenly wanted to get to the end of the story. These memories were bringing up too many complicated feelings.

"Is that when George came into the picture?"

"Yes, he was so handsome and charming. I lost my good sense." Her voice sharpened. "But we're talking about Mary now."

"Sorry, I didn't mean to interrupt." His voice soothed. "Go on with your story."

"Mother Superior told me it was traditional for nuns to take a holy name. That was a relief. Right away I changed my middle name from Agnes to Mary."

He nodded in understanding, then widened his eyes and asked "And what would Mother Mary do now? In your place?"

"Do about what?" She peered into his round, pink face as if searching for clues.

"Do about George."

The muscles in her cheek jerked sideways. She dropped her eyes in confusion. "What can I do about him? I don't know where George is...."

"You almost said where the hell George is, didn't you?" The doctor's eyes caught hers. Their grins were simultaneous. She nodded and flushed.

"You hate not knowing, don't you?"

She nodded again, vigorously. "George is a good-looking old man. Still has his hair. Lots of it. White."

"Well, what do you know." Dr. Furst's voice was flat, neutral. He kept his eyes on her face. She stared at her hands. Neither spoke for a while.

"Do you hate George for leaving you in the dark?"

This time her chin jerked up and down as if in the hands of an angry puppeteer.

"I feel like Punch - no, more like Judy," she said. "Or both,. Like I've been punched."

"And so you have, my good woman. What happens when Judy gets knocked down?"

"She bounces right back up and yells at Punch."

"You want to yell at George, don't you? What would you tell him in your loudest voice?"

"You dirty, lowdown man! You coward!" Her voice rose in pitch and volume.

Dr. Furst glanced around the ward. Everyone was awake now, watching the action. He smiled at the other patients and nodded encouragingly at Margaret Mary.

"You left me in a terrible fix!" she cried.

"And I feel...." he prompted, recalling his psychiatric training in Munich.

"And I hate you! I hate you for being such a coward, for not talking to me, not telling me you were going to leave." She balled her fists and struck the wooden arms of the chair.

"And I hurt...." he whispered, leaning closer so she'd feel his support.

"And I hurt." Her face crumpled. "My heart hurts when you're not beside me." Tears slid down her cheeks and dropped onto the front of her nightgown.

Watching with shiny eyes, Dr. Furst rested a warm hand on the nape of her neck.

Overwhelmed by the tenderness of his touch and the truth of her feelings for George - love and hate all mixed together - she dropped her face into her hands and sobbed.

Dr. Furst lifted his hand and moved back a bit to signal that he honored the depth of her grief and was giving her the space it deserved.

When her weeping had run its course he held out a white handkerchief. She dried her eyes and patted the soft cloth into the damp wrinkles of her cheeks.

"Now, back to Mary," he said gently. "What would your Virgin Mary do about George?"

"Forgive him?" she gulped. "But not yet," she added.

Her voice quavered. "Trust that he's in God's hands."

"Into your hands I commit my spirit," he murmured. "Who said that?"

"Jesus."

"And Margaret Mary? What does she say?" He emphasized the Mary.

She kept her head bowed, eyes and hands in her lap.

"Whose face do you see in your mind's eye?" he asked softly.

"Albert's," she whispered. "My son when he was ten wearing a white smock, carrying a candle. He was an altar boy at Midnight Mass. On Christmas Eve."

+++

*"Oh, Little Town of Bethlehem, how still we see thee lie."* A band of choristers filled the air a little later. They sang their way into the ward, harmonizing in four-part euphony. Nurse Bessie called out names, introducing each patient to each choir member from Grace Gospel Church.

When the carolers lifted into *"Hark, the Herald Angels Sing,"* their cheerful faces reminded Margaret Mary of all the holiday pleasures she had taken for granted for so many years. Her eyes glistened. Dr. Furst squeezed her shoulder in a friendly farewell.

She thanked him with a glance and a nod.
*What would Mother Mary do about George?*
*And what would the Holy Mother do about Albert?*
*What will I do?*

# TEN

☙❧

"When is Epiphany?" she asked as Nurse Bessie collected her tray.

"Why, it begins in just a few hours," responded the nurse. "I'm surprised you're keeping track of Twelfth Night, Mrs. Wright. You're more alert than I thought you were," she added, peering at her patient in a searching way.

Margaret Mary licked her supper spoon to get every last grain of wheat mush. She gazed into its curved surface. Too dull to be much of a mirror, the dented spoon still reflected a spot of light. *Not a star, not by a long shot,* she thought, *but shiny enough to light the way to the manger.*

+++

"You'll survive," said a voice in her head late that night. He sounded foreign, and confident. This made her nervous. She tensed her leg muscles and opened her eyes but could see no one. The ward was dark and still. She listened hard and heard it again. "You will survive."

*Who was that?*

She smelled incense. It put her in mind of High Mass when the priest swung the golden censer. An aromatic smell tickled her nose and made her sneeze. *Frankincense?*

She felt a kind of nervous excitement. Her legs and feet were jiggling under the covers, doing a dance all their own.

"It might hurt," said a murmurous man, a different one. He sounded foreign, too. His words were so indistinct that she could barely make them out. *Sounds like he's talking into his beard.*

"It might hurt," repeated the muted voice, a little louder this time. She didn't like that idea. At the same time she got the sense he was bowing to her. *Bowing? To me?* This idea took some getting used to. She felt both honored and embarrassed.

"It will be hard, but you can do it." Another exotic man spoke after a while. His rounded syllables conveyed courtesy and kindness. *Could these be Wise Men?*

Instead of bracing in fear at such a crazy idea, she noticed a strange sensation. She felt light. Her heart thumped, reminding her of how she felt as a child, skipping rope. Free. Strong. She could not have explained this odd feeling of optimism but sensed something fresh moving through her bloodstream.

The night visitors – *were they really Magi?* - seldom spoke after that but she liked knowing they were nearby. Secure in their company, she felt much too energized to go back to sleep. Her heart pounded as it had when she was ten, a champion jumper in Canada. She felt important all of a sudden, just as she had when the neighborhood girls celebrated her as the winner of the summer jump-rope contest.

*Maybe I do matter.*

She tried on this idea. Lightning didn't strike.

Three foreign men - were they really kings? - remained with her through the night. *Maybe I do matter, if not to George then maybe to God.*

"And to yourself," said a muted voice.

Her heart gave a little lift. She wasn't used to feeling such excitement.

"You can do it," repeated the first man. His tone was musky.

Her heart thudded again. With elation, not fear. Elation was as alien to Margaret Mary as the three night visitors.

Over the years, without noticing it, Margaret Mary had grown suspicious of happiness. She'd learned that doing anything smacking of celebration meant courting bad luck. But tonight there was no getting around it.

*I'm happy.*

This was an astonishing awareness. An epiphany.

She was happy. She lingered with this new gladness, greeting it as a long-lost friend.

*Leo put me here,* she thought, *and I hated that but what I do now, that is up to me.*

"It will be hard, and it might hurt, but you can do it," repeated the first Magi.

"Do what?" she asked.

"Be a friend to others," he replied. "Befriend those who are lost and lonely."

This idea made her eyes fly open. A friend.

Her head nodded. Her arms rose from the blankets, palms lifting toward the night sky. Her wedding ring caught a brief flash of light.

*My illness is over.*

She was certain of it.

A rush of impatience warmed her chest. She thought of apricots hanging from the branch, ripe and juicy. She got a vision of Saint Silvia holding up a silver platter. A lovely bouquet of fruit gleamed on the platter. Golden apricots. Purple plums. Rosy peaches. Come and eat, sang a musical voice. She had never felt such an appetite for life, such eagerness for a New Year to begin.

Just before dawn she rose from bed and felt her way down the dark hall to the communal latrine. The room was little more than a corridor, barely four feet wide and six feet long. The smell of misery saturated the place, had for many decades. Three toilets were separated by temporary strips of lathe. She surveyed the rough pine walls as one might view a coffin.

*My coffin.*

She'd been ready for death dozens of times during the past year. Suddenly the bodily sense of being confined to a coffin struck her as claustrophobic. *I've led a small, pinched life here.* This was a terrifying feeling. It shocked her into a decision.

*I'm done with the sick ward.* She said it aloud, then again. "I am done with this sick ward." Her mind began moving beyond the latrine. "Come, come." She heard the musical voice again. "Come to your new life, fresh and unafraid."

She pictured leaving the infirmary, sliding her hand down the polished bannister, placing her feet on the wide stairs. An image of the front door formed in her mind's eye. She recalled a narrow panel of frosted glass set into the wall alongside the main door of the Manor House. She paused in her reverie, appreciating the honeycomb patterns of moonlight diffused through the glass. The brass doorknob felt cold in her hand. The muscles of her arms moved involuntarily, as if pushing against the heavy oak door. The tendons in her legs jerked of their own accord as she imagined stepping across the threshold and out onto the porch.

It felt good to be outdoors, even in her imagination. She inhaled sharply through both nostrils, taking in the cold, clear air of the winter night.

"Come," beckoned a musky voice. "Come now. It is time to turn loneliness into laughter."

*Twelfth Night. Epiphany.*

# ELEVEN

☙

Three days ago she'd been released from the infirmary. Margaret Mary missed the clean, quiet air. An old steam radiator clanked and blew in the women's ward, which was stifling. The room smelled of old sweat released from the floorboards, of stale breath recycled too many times by too many sad people. She tried to hold her breath, felt in danger of suffocating but finally had to exhale, adding her own moisture to the brew.

The overheated air moved past three old women who puttered around anxiously, reminding her of Esther who had wet her pants right in this spot yesterday. She'd been watching as Esther covered her eyes with both hands while pee trickled down her leg, soaked her carpet slipper and puddled on the floor. Esther wasn't in the room now but the smell remained. It made Margaret Mary yearn to be back in the cool, antiseptic air of the infirmary. She had never expected she'd be homesick for calm nurses and gauzy white curtains. She thought how familiar things imprinted on you. A bed, a scent, a touch. It made her eyes hot. She felt as if her eyes were melting, but melting into what?

She wanted to ask Lily for help but her physical therapist had already helped so much. Margaret Mary couldn't ask again. She wasn't like that.

The hot air flicked across polite conversations as inmates passed the time of day. Such pointless activities seemed now, in this heat, to emit scents of anxiety. For Margaret Mary, the effect was cloying. She limped to the edge of the room, the floor creaking beneath her shoes, and took hold of the wide windowsill. She stood for a moment, gazing out at winter-bare trees, uncertain what to do next. She had returned to the women's ward intending to be friendly and forthright. As she dwelled on the topic of friendliness following the visit of the Magi, it occurred to her that she simply had not tried hard enough. One Wise Man had reminded her of Father who used to say "Having friends meant being friendly."

Two women came into the ward and went out again. She felt awkward in this overheated room, as if she didn't belong. How hard would it be to walk over to Mattie and say in a breezy way, "Hot enough for you?" If she did, these women would see that she was ordinary and pleasant, like them.

But she was not like them. For one thing her husband had dumped her. For another, her sons had left her behind. She had lost her home to the bankers, for a third. She couldn't forget those indignities, all the losses that put her in this godforsaken place. *All the ways I don't matter to the men who matter most to me.*

She crossed her ankles carefully, leaned back against the windowsill and crossed both arms across her ample chest. She didn't fit in here. That was the problem. The women in this ward were all Protestants, for one thing. And they knew how to chit-chat, for another. She wished she had Penny beside her. She missed the silky cocker spaniel, her quizzical eyes, the way she thumped her tail in agreement. She missed how Penny cocked her head, as if asking to hear more. Most of all, Margaret Mary missed feeling important when the dog gazed up at her. She missed feeling as if she mattered to someone.

She looked around the ward with a critical eye, feeling suffocated by dark-stained paneling from floor to ceiling. The tall windows would not open because their frames had warped. The aroma of stale clothing rose to meet Margaret Mary. She longed for a breath of fresh air.

+++

"So, then, what's your new vision?" Lily's tone was abrupt.

"That's just it, I can't see worth a darn." Margaret Mary sounded desperate. "See," she wailed, holding out a pair of wire-rimmed spectacles. The frames were bent out of shape. One lens was missing. "She SAT on them," wailed Margaret Mary, stamping her foot like a child in a temper.

"Did she now? And who is she?" One eyebrow was lifted, and one corner of her mouth, too. Lily's light-heartedness annoyed Margaret Mary.

"Rhoda. She's a new resident, a retired teacher who thinks she knows more than anyone. Meddling is her business. And besides that, she's shaped like a hippopotamus."

"Too bad. Let me take a look."

Margaret Mary handed over the mangled spectacles. Her hand shook.

"Yes, I see the problem. I'm not an oculist, but even I don't see any way to fix these. Tell me, please, why did you come to me? Do I look like a miracle worker?"

"Yes, Lily. You did miracles, teaching me to walk again after I thought I'd spend the rest of my days bedridden. It's due to you that Dr. Furst let me transfer back to the women's ward." She stopped to catch her breath. Drops of sweat were popping out along her hairline.

"Alright, luv, that's enough praise. I can only take little bits at a time, you know."

"So, can you help me? I don't know where else to turn. And besides, I miss you."

Margaret Mary rubbed her hands on the back of her neck. Her outburst left her flustered.

"Ahh, so that's it, eh? Homesick for the old infirmary, are you?" Lily's face crinkled into a wide grin. Seeing three quick nods, she went on. "I just might know someone who can make you a new pair of spectacles. But first, I have a question."

Margaret Mary looked up, puzzled but ready.

"How rich are you?'

"Ohh," she shook her head, "I don't have nearly enough money to buy new glasses."

"That's not the point. I asked how rich you are?"

"I just said…"

"Riches come in many forms. Money is only one."

"Oh. Well then, I'm rich in faith…is that what you mean?"

"Are you rich enough in kindness to help someone who needs it?"

"Help somebody? Why, yes, I think so…maybe … if…"

She stopped, confused.

"If I help get new glasses for you, who will you help?"

"Oh!"

Understanding dawned like sunrise, brightening her eyes. "Oh, you mean sick people? Here? Yes, I think I can do that."

"So, if I arrange for an optician to come and test your eyes, prescribe new lenses and make new frames - at no cost to you - can I count on you to help in the infirmary?"

"Yes, Lily, yes!"

+++

So she made a visit to Rhoda in the infirmary. The clumsy hippo had fallen on the stairs and wound up with a broken hip.

*Serves her right for breaking my glasses*, she thought in an uncharitable moment. *But Lily thinks I'm rich enough in kindness to cheer someone up.* She remembered hearing Hazel Parker tell how it was her duty to call upon the sick when she'd been in the Presbyterian Sunshine Club. So Margaret Mary decided to fulfill her pledge to Lily this very day. She walked calmly to the infirmary, trying on the image of being a gracious Presbyterian lady which, she had heard, was Rhoda's faith, too. She stood patiently at the foot of Rhoda's hospital bed, commenting on the unusually mild weather and the unpredictable infirmary food. All the while, an unpleasant odor was filling the air.

Rhoda appeared overheated. Her forehead glistened, her round cheeks were red and her prominent eyes bugged out. But she talked without pausing about how she missed the women in the ward, at which point Margaret Mary thought to tell her about the fight between Hazel and Jane, about how one had said something rude and the other had slapped an arm. Both had grabbed and pinched at each other until Matron stepped in and made them both put their hands on top of their heads.

Rhoda shook her head, she had heard about this already, and who could believe such a thing, anyway? But the doctor's grown daughter coming here with her woman friend, the both of them traveling all the way from Germany - that was interesting, didn't Margaret Mary think so? Margaret Mary thought so. Amazing, Rhoda said, when you thought about it, two women, both homely as hippos, acting like lovebirds. Rhoda found it all very disturbing.

Margaret Mary, trying not to laugh and tired of nodding, got ready to leave.

"Oh, then..." said Rhoda, "On your way out could you please find Nurse Bessie." She gave Margaret Mary a triumphant nod. "I'm finished with this bedpan now."

Sitting on the porch later, enjoying the sweet, cold air, she could not prevent certain unpleasant images from coming into her mind. It was now obvious, a certain fact, that Rhoda had been using the bedpan throughout her entire visit. Margaret Mary frowned into the clear winter light. It riled her how she had tried her best to act like a Sunshine Club lady. She would tell Hazel, in no uncertain terms, that she wasn't suited for such churchy things. She hated to disappoint Lily but she just wasn't cut out for visiting bedridden patients. No matter how those foreign-sounding night visitors insisted she had a gift for friendliness, she'd have to tell Lily she just wasn't the sunshiny type.

# TWELVE

☙❧

4125 NE 62nd Avenue
Portland, Oregon
February 14, 1936

Dear Mother,
    Your family sends wishes for a Happy Valentine's Day, or at least as happy as it can be when you aren't in your own home. Dean cut out these red hearts for you, and Virginia pasted bits of lace on them to cheer you. Knowing how much you love the color yellow, I'm tucking in a silk scarf to brighten your spirits. Leo thought you'd like it better than something red.

Pastor Evans found these words in an old prayer book and I thought they might bring you a bit of comfort.

This feels like a new day. I don't know what it may bring, but help me be ready.

If I am to stand up, help me to stand steadily.
If I am to sit still, help me to sit quietly.
If I am to lie low, help me to do it patiently.
And if I am to do nothing, let me do it cheerfully. Amen.

Your loving daughter-in-law,
*Cordelia*

# THIRTEEN

☙❧

Bella was a new inmate. She was lonely. And why wouldn't she be? Bella Monelli had felt like a stranger since her husband brought her to this United States. She'd quickly learned that Americans do not like Italians. Neighbor women gossiped about her black clothes and shooed her away when she picked dandelions from their yards. "She makes wine," they whispered, crossing the street to avoid her. Here, in this ward, Bella felt like a stranger among crowds of strangers. She has heard that everyone in this huge house is a pauper.

Bella never did fit in, not since her happy childhood days. In Palermo she'd loved running down the lane, hearing her neighbor singing opera, wondering if today he'd reach the high note of "Vesti la guibba." How free she'd been, skirting the puddles as village women held their wool skirts above the muck. Now I'm trapped in the muck of this Poor Farm, she thought, and I have no idea how to get out.

Misery does not love company. In fact, misery rubs off on others, this she knew. Bella had learned that strangers could do very little about her loneliness. A sigh, a look, even a gesture could spread it. Misery is as contagious as cholera. Knowing this - all too well - Bella went back to bed on a Friday morning. She lay there alone - alone in a bed, alone in a ward, alone on the second story of a brick building. The space was not hers alone, yet she was lonely in it. The bloody smell of iron bed frames and the nightgown odors of strangers crowded in on Bella. The air was suffocating. My world smells like the inside of an old closet, she thought.

She turned over in bed, sliding down hill, deeper into the muck. Rain fell desolately through the winter air and beaded on the windowpane. She pictured the sodden ground, slippery underfoot. Bella resisted the urge to whimper as she watched drops gather and slide down the glass. Water poured from a broken gutter, turning the lawn below into a muddy hole.

She was attached to no one, not since dear Vittorio had died. She produced nothing but bad breath. Bella muttered to herself. She accused herself of cooking up this sadness in order to chew it and swallow it like eggplant parmesana. She imagined herself snipping basil into her sorrow, stirring one lonely chopped pepper into it and simmering everything together into a savory putanesca sauce.

A voice yanked her back from Mama's fragrant kitchen. She did not know what was said or who said it. She felt an unexpected touch, two hands resting lightly on the tops of her feet. Bella glimpsed a round face framed with untidy hair. It pleased her to see the stranger's gray hair was thinning. Warm hands pressed against her feet, making Bella feel unsettled. She looked sideway. Someone was bending from the waist, saying something close to her ear. She pressed her two feet together and made herself concentrate on what the woman was saying.

The visitor leaned down and said it again, "What's the trouble, dear lady?" Her voice was so close that Bella could feel the vibration in her ear. Her cheek sensed the roundness of Margaret Mary's breath, the voice of one woman touching the skin of another.

"What's the matter? Can you tell me about it? I'd like to hear what's troubling you."

Suddenly, in that moment, Bella decided she was tired of being lonely. *Misery is making me sick,* she thought. Pushing back the covers and sitting up on the edge of her bed, she patted the mattress and invited Margaret Mary to rest beside her. In thyme-scented Italian, the newest stranger at the Poor Farm began to pour out tangled tales of love and money. Hugging her forearms across her heart, she told of romance and marriage, of love found and lost again. Her fingers twisted to show the complexity of her situation. She rocked back and forth as she told of being poor, then rich enough to immigrate, telling her story of money lost, found, and lost again.

She told of learning to speak English after a ship's mate advised her to learn all the words she could. Bella's husband found work for them on an Oregon farm. She talked to everyone there, to the other laborers as they worked together spreading manure from wheelbarrows, weeding onions and pulling carrots. She talked while hilling potatoes and tamping dirt. Bella clenched her hands and flexed her biceps to show Margaret Mary all the farm labor she'd done. She kept on learning, adding more American words while scything, raking and shocking hay. Eventually she could say most of what she wanted to say, and most people could understand.

Bella talked on and on, gesturing like an actress, waving the sleeves of her tattered nightgown. The start of an aria twitched in her mouth. Clearing her throat of accumulated silence, Bella Monelli sang out bits of opera. Margaret Mary nodded and listened. She didn't understand all the words, but she did understand the pain of loneliness. Nodding, smiling and occasionally patting the woman's hand, she listened with all her heart. The alert expression on her face encouraged more stories. At the end, Bella hugged her forearms and rocked from side to side. Some of the happier parts of herself were revived. She celebrated by humming another aria.

+++

"At least I am alive," said Margaret Mary. It was Lent. She had told Bella about her long, dark year in bed. They decided to count their blessings out loud.

"At least I'm not the only stranger here," said Bella.

"At least the Holy Family keeps watch over us," said Margaret Mary, overjoyed to have another Catholic in the ward.

"At least I'm fed and warm this winter."

"At least half of my face doesn't droop like Emma's."

"At least I wasn't on The Titanic."

"At least not much of my hair is falling out."

"At least the gray tabby cat curled up on my lap yesterday."

"Amen," they finished in unison.

+++

"Mama's name was Olivetta. Her hobby was going to wakes," said Bella one windy afternoon. "Most of all, she loved going to First Saturday Sorrowful Mother Novenas."

"Sounds like she made the best of death in traditional Italian style," laughed Margaret Mary. "I had a great-aunt whose hobby was going to cemeteries. She taught me how to decorate a grave."

"Well, that gives us another thing in common. Mama taught me how to bend over an open casket and firmly press the hand of the corpse while mumbling a prayer."

"Why would she do a thing like that?"

"She said she did it to feel more like a part of the family."

"You mean she attended wakes for people she didn't know? Squeezed the hands of strangers?"

"Yes, and made me to do it, too, from when I was little. I was squeamish at first, but after a while I began to enjoy myself. In Palermo they served great food at wakes."

Margaret Mary raised her eyebrows extravagantly. Bella grinned, touched her gold hoop earring with one finger, then went on.

"My mother fancied that she would meet a new husband at a wake. She was widowed young, you know, and had been waiting for the right man for almost twenty years."

"Did Mr. Right ever come along?"

"Not for her, but I met my husband at a wake." She got a far-away look in her eyes.

"Tell me more," grinned Margaret Mary.

"I always got so sentimental at wakes. During Mr. Dolan's, this sturdy man moved close and patted my back until I stopped sobbing. Then he gave me a wink. Vittorio was his name. He was wearing a starched white shirt with four rosaries click-clacking around his neck. I couldn't take my eyes off the man."

"Isn't that funny," sighed Margaret Mary. "George slid into my pew one hot morning and swept me off my feet, too. That marked the end of my days in the convent." She let out another deep sigh. They'd been over this topic before. Bella changed the subject.

"Want to see my collection of holy cards?"

"Yes, I guess…" It was hard for Margaret Mary to shake off thoughts of George. Bella knew this although they'd not been acquainted for long.

"My mother was a permanent widow. She kept the rooms in our house dark and hung black crepe over the portrait of my father. His face looked so startled, probably because he died so young. I was only two."

Margaret Mary nodded sympathetically. Bella went on. "If Mother had a headache, she would hold a holy card against her forehead and put a statue of St. Sebastian in her lap. You know, he's the saint with twenty-four arrows sticking out of his body."

Margaret Mary didn't, but nodded anyway. "Where'd you get so many holy cards?"

"At wakes, like I said. I collected as many as I could from all the holy card tables. I like this one, don't you?" She handed over a card of St. Patrick standing on a snake. Margaret Mary shuddered and dropped it back into the red velvet box. Snakes made her nervous.

She fingered one depicting a woman.

"That's Blessed Saint Silvia," explained Bella. "She spooned waxy honey from the comb, spread it on bread and gave it to hungry people."

"I like honey better than snakes. And you know, when I was in the infirmary I think I remember Saint Silvia bringing me apricots on a fancy platter."

"Yes, the silver platter is her symbol. She's famous for arranging fresh fruits and vegetables on silver platters and giving them to her son Gregory. Silvia was so generous-hearted she didn't even fuss when her son gave away her silver to ragged beggars."

"She sounds like a saint," murmured Margaret Mary. "After George left, I had to pawn my mother's silver candlesticks to buy food for Penny-dog."

"Saint Silvia would forgive you," said Bella, holding up another holy card. "Now, here's the one I need these days, Blessed Arnaldo of Padua. He's good for arthritis pains."

# FOURTEEN

☙❧

She took a chair at the end of the porch and gazed up at the high overcast. Sometimes the clouds looked bruised, but today they seemed serene. A twisted old man sat at the other end of the porch, his face a ruin of living. Margaret Mary had seen him before. Neither made eye contact or acknowledged the other. Privacy was an unspoken courtesy between strangers whose destitute condition had landed them at the Poor Farm.

*What is a stranger, exactly? The Bible says welcome the stranger, but I was taught not to speak to strangers. Especially men. Are strangers in the Manor House different than strangers on the streets of Portland? Does eating and sleeping in close quarters make a difference? If we're not exactly strangers, then what are we?*

One thing about Edgefield, there were plenty of strangers to watch and plenty of conversations to overhear. Not that she thought of herself an eavesdropper, exactly. Her mother hated eavesdroppers and had severely punished Margaret Mary for listening to grown-up talk but she did like to listen.

*If God didn't want people to listen in on each other* she thought *He would have put ear-lids on humans.* Since she couldn't shut out other peoples' voices, she figured it wasn't a sin to listen. She liked personal stories, always had. All these strangers who wound up under the Manor House roof provided grist for her story mill.

Margaret Mary had an active imagination. Behind us, she said to herself, looms the Manor House, its grandeur blunted by time. Black mold is growing in the cracks of the wooden window frames. The man with the bent back is gazing at the distant hills, lost in thought. Wind, rain and frost had laid waste to the structures of this old building, just as poverty and sadness are laying waste to that old man's life. And to mine. Her thoughts wandered, losing the thread of the stranger's story and moving into the familiar weave of her own family drama. It was enough to depress anybody.

+++

Near the end of April a letter came from Montana. It arrived on a Monday, cold and overcast. Trees were beginning to leaf out, pale green against the barren sky. She had just come from the infirmary, from visiting Hazel who had pleurisy. Margaret Mary leaned against the front desk to read her brother's letter.

Billings, Montana
April 22, 1936

Dear Margaret Mary,

Well, sister, it has been a long time. You know I'm not much of a letter writer but a surprise limped up the back steps last week. Yep, it was your husband George, all ratty and stinking of gin. He'd been riding the rails with a bunch of sorry hobos. Got as far as Billings before he took sick, then hitched a ride out to our ranch on a neighbor's stock truck. He's a sorry sight, that's for sure. Says he wants to stay and work if we'll have him. Says he'll muck out the stables, feed the stock and do the chores in exchange for a place to flop, three squares and a bit of tobacco. I was ready to boot his smelly butt off the place, but you know how softhearted Ellen is. She'd take in Al Capone if he turned up as weak and woe-be-gone as old George. So we'll look after him for a while. Your no-good husband is in good hands for now, at least.

He's not much of a talker as you know - neither am I - but from what Ellen got out of the guy it sure sounds like you got the raw end of the deal. Pretty piss-poor way to treat a woman, and I've said that to his dirty face. I'd say it even if you weren't my big sister.

Wish I could help out but things are tight here, too. I'll slip a little cash in the envelope and hope it helps.

I told George I was sending a letter your way and asked if he had anything he wanted to tell you. He didn't.

Wish things were better for you, Sis, but I know your faith is strong. If anyone can churn sour milk into butter, it's you.

Keep your chin up and keep in touch,
   Your brother,  *James Robert Doig*

+++

Sitting on the edge of her bed and reading James' letter over and over again, she felt tears well up. Her younger brother was such an awkward man. They'd never been close. He'd never written her a letter before. Come to think of it, she'd never written to him either. It took her a week to think what to say. She wrote it on a postcard.

James, thanks for looking after George but you don't have to send me money. Your sister, *Margaret Mary*

His reply came a week later.
I don't need you to tell me what to do.
   Your brother, *James*.
There wasn't much of an answer for that.

She was still dithering over what to say to George, or whether to write to him at all.

"It'll get better," Bella said sympathetically when she saw tears brimming in Margaret Mary's eyes. "You'll feel better before long. Time helps," she smiled, patting her friend's arm. "Time always helps."

+++

The next afternoon, Margaret Mary was in the women's sitting room with a *Saturday Evening Post* open on her lap, staring out the window. Clouds scudded along, pushed by the eastern wind. It surprised her, somehow, to see ordinary Oregon weather on a day such as this. She pulled her brown sweater close and buttoned it across her aching heart.

*Oh, it was sad. It wasn't right that George and I were so far apart. My husband had been scared, too, hadn't he?* She found it bewildering to realize how a woman could frighten a man without even knowing it. She'd always figured she was a thoughtful wife. Conscientious.

It was even more terrible to think she'd been a poor mother. Margaret Mary's foot was bobbing quickly, in tiny little jerks. She had tried to do the right thing with Albert, raised him the best she knew how. But she had regrets, secret regrets. Her son had needed strictness. She knew that now. She had not been strict enough with him. All the love in the world couldn't prevent the awful truth. She had failed Albert, failed him in too many ways to count.

+++

*Dear George,* she composed in her head. *Many months have passed and I've been worried about you. I hope this letter finds you returning to good health. I don't know where Albert has gone, don't know what has become of our son...*

Margaret Mary rewrote her letter to George many times that week and mailed it the following Monday. After that there was nothing to do but wait. Every few days Bella would ask if she'd received a reply. It was a terrible thing to wait for a letter.

Each day formed around a morning of hopefulness, an afternoon's eager anticipation and the evening's fog of disappointment. How odd it felt, this empty waiting, like stones of rejection dropping into a bottomless pool, sending out circles of speculation. *Maybe the post office lost the letter. Maybe it was dissolving in a puddle beneath some bridge. Maybe George didn't live with her brother's family any more. But James or Ellen would write and tell me, wouldn't they?*

After a while, Bella stopped mentioning it.

At night Margaret Mary sometimes yearned for him, remembering George as he had been to her. Important. Handsome. Someone to love. She still wanted someone to love. If her husband should appear in this room, touch the back of her neck and whisper sweet words in her ear, she knew she would throw her arms around him. But of course George Albert Wright did not appear. The silence of her unanswered letter remained tense, unchanged.

# FIFTEEN

☙❧

Several times during the spring of 1936, she felt free while sitting on the porch. Free, simply free. There was no other way to put it. It was like seeing the sun come out after a wild winter storm. Her mind felt clear, the way air smells after a rain. She was free of fear. How strange, to not be frightened. These feelings of freedom took her by surprise. They didn't last long, but they gave her a sense of warmth toward the people around her. She still had nothing, no money, that is. She had eyes to watch the sparrows, but no money to feed them.

It was time to make a new life for her self, but she didn't know how. She could imagine a day when she would hoist herself up and move in a new direction, but she couldn't figure out what she would do differently. Then a flock of swallows would veer off in a different direction and disappear from view, and her sense of freedom would disappear, too. There she'd sit, like a bump on a log, worrying about the whereabouts of her second son or fussing with herself about how she could become less of a stranger around here. Wondering if George would ever answer her letter.

Sometimes, gazing at the starry sky, she would think about praying, because she had not prayed for a long time. She could not do that now, so she did nothing. It was not that she'd given up on the Good Lord or the Holy Mother. Not that they had given up on her, either. It was more that she was wandering around in some large, baffling confusion. She simply could not sort things out.

+++

June 10, 1936

Ten things to do on a rainy day

1. Mend my brown dress
2. Sort my keepsakes
3. Get acquainted with Benjamin, the new watchmaker
4. Sit under the eaves and watch the rain
5. Visit with Betty, the cheery mail clerk
6. Go to the laundry and fold linens
7. Read *The Lives of the Saints*
8. See what Hazel is up to
9. Take a nap
10. See if Ben Borden can repair my golden chain

# SIXTEEN

☙❧

Her golden neck chain was broken, the delicate one with the little cross on it. George had surprised her a few years back, fixing it around her neck in a brief, romantic moment. It was the only bit of gold she owned except for the thin wedding ring on her left hand. She missed being able to wear the chain with its pretty cross. She'd heard about a new watchmaker, Benjamin Borden, who'd set up his workbench in the basement. Maybe he would know how to put a new clasp on her gold chain. She wrapped it carefully in a handkerchief and prepared to find out.

Margaret Mary wanted to make a good impression. She cast an eye on her corset but decided against it. Nothing could contain these wide hips. She brushed her unruly hair and tied a bright yellow scarf around her neck to hide the wrinkles. Her treasured bottle of Evening in Paris cologne was nearly empty but she dabbed a whiff behind one ear. In the hallway she passed Henry Bellows, the bearded boot-maker. *What a funny name for such a quiet, shy man.* When she said hello he ducked his chin, barely nodding in response. *He hardly makes a peep, let alone a bellow,* she thought.

She made her way carefully down the stairs to the basement of the Manor House. Placing both feet firmly on each step, she gripped the rail with one hand and hung her cane loosely over the other. Pay attention now, she cautioned herself. Slowly, she moved past a stack of suitcases and craned her neck to see what Benjamin Borden was doing. She paused for breath as a flutter of excitement rippled beneath her camisole, warming her cheeks. She peeked around some supply barrels and spied a sparrow-sized man illuminated by the bare bulb hanging from a rafter above his worktable. He was intent upon on the collection of tiny sprockets and springs spread before him. A jeweler's monocle covered the eye nearest to Margaret Mary so she could see him without being seen. This suited her just fine. She was jumpy all of a sudden and wanted time to take stock of this attractive new resident.

*It looks as if he is assembling the innards of a lady's watch,* she thought. *What small hands he has, and what narrow wrists.* In the clear light shining onto his workbench she observed the glisten of his short, clean nails and the curl of fine white hairs on the backs of his hands. The watchmaker's slender fingers fascinated her. *He seems to be concentrating so hard. Do I dare disturb him?*

Her reverie was broken when two men came clattering down the stairs. She recognized Mr. BB Jackson, Superintendent of the Manor House. He was a man who could control any number of situations. Out of his hearing, some of the inmates referred to him as Big Boss. *I do not want to cross his path this morning*, she thought, stepping deeper into the shadows. *I'm not even sure an ordinary person like me is allowed in the basement.*

"This way, sir," said Mr. Jackson. Despite his beefy build, he moved quickly across the cement floor. The other big fellow had to step lively to keep up. "Here's where your watchmaker has set up shop." The Superintendent turned to address a meaty man with heavy eyebrows, dressed in dark suit, vest and tie. "Mr. Borden," boomed Jackson, "let me introduce Mr. Thomas Ingraham. Of the Portland Ingrahams." When the visitor held out his hand his suit coat strained across his back.

She held her breath as Mr. Ingraham grasped the watchmaker's delicate hand with such force it made Ben grimace.

"Careful there," Ben warned. "These are the only hands I've got." Then, with a gaze light as smoke, he added "Pleased to meet you, Mister Ingraham."

"Thank you for showing me the way to Mr. Borden's shop," the visitor said to the manager. "I will find my own way out."

She noted the sharp tone of dismissal. Mr. Jackson was usually the one to dismiss underlings. Today he was dismissed abruptly but simply nodded, said "You are welcome, sir." It sounded to Margaret Mary as if he took the stairs three at a time.

"What brings you here?" Ben asked mildly.

"A bit of city business." Ingraham paused. Their eyes met and held. The brawny man was first to look away, turning his gaze in her direction. Margaret Mary froze in case the man spotted her hiding place, but he was so intent on his business that he didn't notice her behind the crates. *Stay real still,* she cautioned herself. *No time for a cough.* She steadied her stance, lightened her breath and listened with all her might.

"City business, you say. And what might that be, Mister Ingraham?"

"You have a reputation in Portland as a responsible businessman, Mr. Borden. But we have not met before and I need to ask. Can I trust you?"

"Who am I being asked to trust, sir? I need to know your business before we go any further." Benjamin Borden's tone was as cool as silver.

"The Ingraham family owns the pawnshop at Second and Broadway..." The visitor cleared his throat and went on. "Our store has been in the family since 1907. Folks bring things in to pawn and..."

"Might any of these things be stolen?" Ben interrupted in a tone sharp as a pick.

"Well, hmmmpphhh..."

Ingraham swallowed so hard that Margaret Mary heard him gulp from ten feet away.

"Mister Ingraham, let me be perfectly clear. My reputation is based on integrity. I will not receive or repair stolen watches. Is that understood?"

"Well..."

"Good day, Mister Ingraham. Godspeed."

Ben turned back to the watch parts laid out on his bench. The visitor coughed nervously, brushed cobwebs from one sleeve then trod heavily toward the stairwell. Ben watched him go. His clear gaze caught Margaret Mary's as her eyes shined from the shadows.

"What have we here?" he asked, sounding both surprised and amused. She stepped into the light and moved in Ben's direction.

"Wasn't that something!" she blurted. "I couldn't help overhearing."

"And what did you hear, my good lady?"

"I heard an honest man tell a shady one that he refused to be part of any dirty business," she said. Benjamin's smile gave her the confidence to go on. "A man I would like to get to know," she added quickly.

"And who might you be?" he asked in a courtly manner.

So began a new chapter in the life of an old lady.

# SEVENTEEN

☙❧

Ben and Margaret Mary were strolling in the lavender light, talking of this and that, when they heard shouts from the far side of the barn.

"What's that?" She was more curious than frightened.

"Sounds like a bunch of rowdy men," he said.

They paused. He glanced at her. She nodded. He grasped her elbow and they changed direction, moving in unison toward the din.

Beyond the barn, two ranch hands in dirt-stiffened overalls were dragging their boot heels through the muck while others shouted. Men with raw, hoarse voices yelled "Bigger, there, fellas." "Come on Al, you can make it bigger than that."

"It looks like they're digging a circle in the barnyard," she whispered. "Why would they be doing a thing like that?"

"Let's watch and see," Ben said. "Some of those guys look like bad business."

Rangy men with sun-dark faces called out jokes she didn't understand. Farmhands with white foreheads leaned against the rail fence, hooting in coarse voices. "Their day's work is done," she observed, "and now they can enjoy themselves."

"It may not be that simple," he said. Ben stood tense beside her in the barn shadows. "Yes, they plow the fields and harvest the grain that feeds us all," he murmured, "but they may be getting up to no good."

"Coin toss time!" a man shouted. She couldn't see who it was, evidently someone with authority, because most of the others quit pushing and began digging in their pockets.

"That's right, fellas. Toss in all you've got." Pennies and nickels began flying through the air and landing in the circle. The ranch hands were so involved in frisking their pockets and tossing their coins that no one noticed two old folks watching. Ben tucked Margaret Mary's hand under his arm and raised an eyebrow in her direction. She shook her head, puzzled about what was going on.

"Hold off for a minute, fellas." The leader of this odd game held up both hands, waited for the sprinkle of coins to stop, then stepped across the line. He bent down and picked up an array of pennies, nickels and dimes from the dirt.

"There's one quarter here, too" he announced, holding it high in the fading light. "Thanks, fellas, keep 'em coming." A few men tossed more coins.

"Hey Will, help me count," he called. A stringy man in worn boots and a red-plaid shirt made a show of hopping over the line and holding out both hands, palms up. The head man counted aloud as he dropped money into Will's hands. "85, 90, 92 cents ... Thanks, fellas, but that's not enough for a jug of muscatel. Dig deeper or none of us will get any booze tonight." A chorus of grumbles rose around the circle.

"Give us a break, Lex," someone complained. "I'm down to my last dime here."

"Toss it in, man, we're all counting on you."

A few coins later Lex yelled "Give me a drum roll, I think we've got it." Three of the ranch hands beat on their denim thighs and mouthed percussive sounds. Drums gave way to cheers when Cox announced "One dollar and 35 cents, my good men. We made it." Cheers drowned out his next words.

Lex waved his arms to get the crowd's attention. "Who'll walk with me to Troutdale to buy a jug of wine?" Three rowdy guys shoved into the circle, punching shoulders.

"All right, the rest of you suckers gonna wait here for the party to start?"

"Not a chance, Lex," someone yelled back. "I don't trust you as far as I can throw your skinny ass."

"C'mon, men, let's all go with him," called a toughened voice. With that, a dozen workingmen shook off their tiredness and headed for the railroad tracks, the quickest route to Troutdale.

"So that's why they drew that circle in the dirt," said Margaret Mary.

"Yes, my dear, "grinned Ben. "And that's why they'll wake me up in the middle of the night, stumbling into the ward, bumping into beds and tripping over feet. Aren't you glad you won't have to smell these guys in a few hours?"

"Men," she said, with a half-smile and a small shake of her gray head.

"Men, indeed," he agreed, taking her arm. "But make sure you steer clear of those two ruffians in the plaid shirts. They could be trouble."

+++

But the weather was perfect. "Perfect weather," the women in the ward said to each other, shaking their heads in amazement. The evening sky was vast and lavender-blue, the fields vibrant with tender shoots of grain. Margaret Mary, back from her walk with Ben, stood at the window beside her bed. She loved how long the late June evenings had become.

Poking through her trunk (George's old Army trunk) looking for nothing in particular, she found herself thinking of Benjamin Borden's small and slightly tilted mouth. She wondered what it would be like to press her lips against it. She was certain that no one had kissed him in years. *Older people tended not to kiss much,* she thought.

Just then Bella yelled. "Have you seen my black sweater? The one with the silver buttons?" Perhaps, Margaret Mary considered uncharitably, Bella was losing her eyesight, or her memory. In addition to that, her dentures smelled awful.

"Under the corner of your bed," she answered. "And for heaven's sake, don't shout."

Bella switched to Italian, mouthing what sounded like curses, but at least she lowered the volume. Margaret Mary, feeling a bit more generous, poked her cane beneath the other woman's bed and raked the missing black sweater out into the aisle. Bella - still muttering - bent to pick it up. She shot a dark look at Margaret Mary and shook the dusty sweater in her direction.

"And for goodness sake, don't wave that dirt at me," she complained mildly, but her heart wasn't in it. She wasn't in the mood for a fight, not with pink and violet streaking the evening sky. Sending a conciliatory half-smile in Bella's direction, Margaret Mary brushed a few loose strands of hair from her face. She stood at the window watching the sparrows dipping under the eaves, wondering when their eggs would hatch. Or had the baby birds already broken out of their shells when she wasn't watching?

She sniffed her fingertips and caught the fragrance of crushed sweet peas. *Gifts from God,* she thought, picturing again the tender mouth of Ben. Her gaze rested on Bella, head bent, brushing one hand across her wool sweater. *Baby sparrows. Long lovely lilac twilights. They were all gifts of God, even Bella, who will probably fart in her sleep again as she does most nights. Everything is a gift from the Good Lord.*

# EIGHTEEN

❧※☙

The weather was still kind. As she rested on the porch, Margaret Mary noticed a faint smell of manure drifting up from the barn. The tall brick Manor House still didn't feel like home although she had been sleeping in a cot on the second story for half a year now. She found a chair and dropped her wide hips into it, moving the rocker back and forth with her good foot. The rhythm was soothing.

Her gaze fell on a man in dirty work boots, walking with an awkward gait. His legs were long and thin but he moved like a boy not yet at home in his man's body. Something about him made her want to give a kind word.

"Good afternoon," she called to the young farmhand.

He stumbled to a stop.

"Afternoon, ma'am." His pale blue eyes were level with her hazel ones. Their gaze met across a banister that stood six steps above the ground. He lifted a broken straw hat from reddish curls and tipped it toward Margaret Mary with a stiff little half-bow from the waist. She smiled warmly and nodded back.

"Watcha doin?" He nodded his chin quick as a bee.

"What am I doing this fine afternoon?" she repeated to buy a little time. *He seems like a nice enough boy, if a little slow in the head.* She decided to risk being playful.

"Why, I am enjoying some little hurricanes here as I take the summer air. Would you care to join me?"

"Huh?" He looked around in confusion. "Where's thuh... huh...hurry-cane?"

"Do you see those purple hollyhocks?"

He turned to follow her gesture, nodding vigorously.

"Do you see the bees busy at their centers?"

"Yup, them's honeybees."

"I call them hurricanes but you know their true name. Are you a beekeeper here at the farm?"

"Oh no, missus. The boss wanted me to learn how 'ta work the hives, ona count of my name starts with B, but I'ma skeered of them bees."

*Why, that was a whole sentence, and most of it made sense. Margaret Mary was enjoying this. In fact, I do believe this is the first time in my life I have dared to talk to someone who isn't right in the head,* she thought. *Why, if George or Leo were here they would scowl.* She got a sudden vision of her men sending this boy running one way and hurrying her in the other direction. *But they aren't here now, are they. And I can chat with this tall, skinny drink of water if I like.*

"Yes. You know, I'm a bit scared of bees myself, especially when they get close, but I rather enjoy watching from a distance as they gather nectar from hollyhocks."

No reply. His back was turned toward the flowers.

"Bees aren't always busy working," she said with a smile. "Sometimes they're playing." No answer. He was probably trying to see her little hurricanes.

"Ahem. You said your name starts with B. Is it Bob?"

"No, ma'am. Guess again."

"Bill?"

"Nope."

"Bradley?"

That brought a giggle from him, along with a shake of his damp curls.

"Benton?" *Where in the world did that come from?*

Another happy head shake. His lips opened in a wide, spit-damp grin. She could see his big shiny teeth.

"Battalion Chief?" She was almost giddy all of a sudden.

"Nuh, nuh, NO!" he announced. "It's BUSTER!"

"Oh, Buster, I am so happy to meet you. My name is Margaret Mary."

"Muh...mug...mugrit...y" he stammered, "muh...murry!"

"But you can call me MMMM," she added quickly. "By my initials. How about that?"

"Huh-llo, UMMMM," he repeated, with another funny little half-bow.

"No need to bow, Buster. I am not the queen, you know."

This got them laughing until he was smacking his hat against his bony thigh, sending bits of straw lifting on the breeze. She was gasping, hugging herself around the waist.

"Oh, my...." Margaret Mary wheezed... "oh me, oh my, I haven't had such a good laugh for I don't know how long."

"Me, too," said Buster, leaning both elbows on his thighs and fanning has pink face with what was left of the hat.

"I do believe we have sent this old chair right off its rockers," she added. The mention of rockers set them off again into what she would later describe to Ben and Bella as hurricanes of laughter.

+++

A few afternoons later Buster came by as Margaret Mary sat on the shady porch enjoying the breeze. He clumped up the steps as he sang "Huh-loo there UMMM."

"It is so good to see you, Buster." She spoke with a sudden lift of delight. She saw something in his hand.

"What have we here?"

"Ah liddle...thuh...thuh..thang...." he stammered.

"A thang...... fer... yer cane." He ran out of words.

Margaret Mary couldn't see what was hidden inside his big callused hand.

"Here' Ah'll show ya..."

He opened his palm to reveal a little black bit of something. It looked like rubber. As he picked it up in his long fingers, a feeling of reverence washed over her, the way she once felt when the priest at St. Mary's held up a communion wafer. With a small bow, Buster reached for her cane, then pulled his hand back. He sought Margaret Mary's eyes with his own and raised both reddish eyebrows as if to ask "May I?"

"Please." She nodded permission.

It must be said that Margaret Mary's dear old cane had become a source of humiliation to her. It made far too much noise when she navigated the bare plank hallways in this home she now shared with many people. The original rubber tip had worn out so long ago, she couldn't remember what it was like to tread softly. The raw metal tip of her cane made an awful whack each time it hit the floor.

*This boy must have noticed my embarrassment and decided to make a new one.* Margaret Mary's heart expanded so big it was a wonder her bony old chest could hold it.

Something about Buster reminded her of Father Finnegan. Not the way he talked, for sure. More the way he touched. The young man lifted her cane in two hands, holding it up to the light, gazing at it like it was a holy chalice or something. Then he wrapped one hand around it and used the other for balance as he lowered his long body down onto the porch. Buster's touch on her cane was so tender, Margaret Mary felt a salty prick behind her eyes. A few tears leaked as she watched the young farmhand carefully fit a small rubber tip onto the end of her cane, as tenderly as if he was handling the sanctified host. She hardly drew a breath, nor did he, until Buster got it right. He pounded the end of the cane on the concrete a few times to secure it.

"Where did you get that?" she asked.

"Nuh..uh..didn't get it," he said. "Uh...uh...MADE it."

"Made it?" She didn't understand.

"Yuh...from an old bit of tire."

"Where in the world did you get a tire?"

"From the shop....the old farm truck."

"How did you make this?"

"Jericho showed me...which tools ta use..."

"Who's Jericho?"

"Big man...black man...in thuh cobbler shop..."

"How did you know?..." This time Margaret Mary was the one who ran out of words.

"Jus saw ya...." said Buster, looking down. His face was red.

"Thank you, Buster. You are so thoughtful. Thank you very much...my...my friend."

"Yer weh-come...muh...friend..." he said, bowing from the neck.

"Now remember what I said about bowing and rockers," she said. They were laughing so hard neither noticed a nurse and two clerks crowding into the doorway to hear what was so funny.

# NINETEEN

☙❧

"So you're the one with the same initials as mine." Margaret Mary addressed a woman standing beside her at the desk where mail was delivered. Not that she got letters very often, but she checked every day just in case George decided to reply.

"I noticed a new name on the box beside mine, now here you are." She smiled tentatively, waiting for a response.

The short black woman glanced up. She took in Margaret Mary's rounded frame leaning to the left on a cane. She noticed laugh lines fanning out from merry eyes.

"That is right. I am new here. My name is Mabel May Wood." She put equal emphasis on each syllable.

"Pleased to meet you. I am Margaret Mary Wright, but my friend calls me UMMMM."

"Now why would she do that?"

"He. Buster. Works in the barn. He's a sweet young man who stammers his words so I told him he could just call me by my initials, MMMM."

"Hmmmm..." The fudge-skinned woman turned aside to hide a quick grin.

"How do you like it here, Mabel May?"

"Well I can't hardly find my way around these long halls, and haven't met a soul yet... except you..."

"Would you like me to show you around?"

"I would enjoy that."

"Do you like to pick blackberries?" *Where did that come from?* Margaret Mary was startled by her own boldness.

"Why, yes, indeed I do," answered Mabel May quickly, letting loose with a wide grin. Her black eyes gleamed with anticipation.

"Let's start our tour with the dining hall," said Margaret Mary. "That's the most important room to me. Then we'll go to the kitchen and ask if they'll lend us two tin pails. The cooks like fresh berries. I'll show you my favorite blackberry patch. It's not far."

"Pleased, I am sure," agreed Mabel May. "But before we go, let me put on a long-sleeved shirt. This dark skin of mine gets sunburned more easily than you might think."

"Why, I never thought of that," said Margaret Mary. "I always figured sunburn was only a problem for folks with pale Scottish skin."

"I can see you have a lot to learn from people of my color," grinned Mabel May. Her voice sounded scolding, but her smile was soft.

+++

A few days later, Buster came by the porch where Margaret Mary was rocking in the shade. It was his third visit this week. This time he skipped the greetings to get right to his mission. "D'ya want I should fix that shoe a'yern?" he blurted.

"Fix it how?" She looked down at her worn black oxfords.

"Ya know....make it taller at the heel fer ya..."

Buster held two slim fingers an inch apart, shifting from words to gestures.

"Oh," she said, getting the picture. *He must mean to make the left shoe higher somehow, to make both my legs the same length.*

"Why, Buster, that is a fine idea. But how could you do it?"

"Well, missus, I'd take yer shoe out to thuh....thuh barn and..."

"Wait, you'd take my shoe away? But it's the only pair I have..."

"Jericho....sez...Uh......" He stopped in confusion.

"Well...yes...uh..." Now she was stammering. Buster's speech pattern was contagious.

He raised his chin as if to look at her, then ducked again and picked nervously at a scab on his knuckle.

"Tell me, Buster, do you know how to fix shoes like mine?"

"No, ma'am .....nuh...nut yet..."

"Oh, dear me..."

"But, missus ... Jericho said....he towld me ....he'd hep me cut and glue..."

"Oh Buster, you are a sweet man but ... but you see, I have just this one pair of shoes. If you take one to the barn I shall have no way to walk..."

"Jericho, he sed, he towld me....Uh'd make a good cobbler... some day. He...he sez Uh....Uh... have a GIFT."

Buster blushed, ducked his head and scuffed one size 12 boot against the other.

"Oh dear, I want you to have a chance to learn, but .... Oh, I'm sorry, Buster, I just can't."

+++

A young Negro woman with a dust rag walked into the sitting room just as Margaret Mary and Mabel May were settling into chairs by the window. The girl wore a checkered apron around her round middle and a white headscarf around her wooly hair. There was a gap between her front teeth and red rims around her eyes. One eye was bright brown, the other clouded. She bumped into a chair as she crossed the room. She swished a ragged undershirt across the mantel, looking in their direction instead of at her work. The girl's behavior was distracting. Margaret Mary was itching to tell Mabel May about Buster and the shoe. She had so many mixed feelings that she didn't know where to start. She figured her new friend had more than a pocket full of common sense and could help sort out her confusion.

"Hey, girl, what's your name?" asked Mabel May.

"Florrie." Her voice was wispy as dandelion fluff.

"Speak up, girl. No need to be nervous."

"Florrie." This time the girl's voice had more starch in it.

"What's wrong with your eye?"

"Got hit in it."

"Hit, how?"

*Mabel May sure is a bold one,* thought Margaret Mary. *Time to put in my two cents.*

"Come on over here and sit with us, Florrie," she invited. "Are you new here?"

"Yes'm, I came yestiday. Got me a bed up in the attic with some kitchen girls."

"Does your eye hurt much?"

"No ma'am. It happened long time ago. Some mean boys pelted me with rocks when I was just a little one."

"Do you have any sisters?" asked Mabel May, giving the girl a squinty look.

"Yes'm, I got six. I'm the youngest. One helped chase those boys away."

"And the others?" asked Margaret Mary.

"The others gave me a hard time 'til we got parceled out to different aunties. Then times got real hard and I wound up here."

"Didn't we all," murmured Margaret Mary.

"Where do you come from?" She didn't mind probing.

"North Portland, near Albina," said Florrie.

"Well, mercy sakes, so did I," blurted Margaret Mary.

"That makes three of us," said Mabel May with a big grin. "Imagine that!"

+++

So began an unlikely alliance. The milk-skinned lady with thinning gray hair would not have said a word to these chocolate-skinned women if they'd met in their old neighborhood. But sharing tables and tasks at the Poor Farm offered common ground, a fresh opening. Three females - one white and two black - stepped through it that day to begin forging a surprising new friendship.

Margaret Mary's dilemma started things off. She was too frazzled to keep it to herself. Florrie and Mabel May heard her whole tale. They thought it best to meet Jericho Taylor, so all three women trooped down to the barn. That went well. Mabel May's crisp questions raised up all of Margaret Mary's concerns. The man's answers erased her doubts. Once the cobbler assured them that he would supervise Buster very closely, and promised to get Margaret Mary's left shoe back on her foot by suppertime, the decision was made.

When Jericho announced it, Buster jiggled with excitement. Enthusiasm must have been second nature to him. He hopped from one foot to the other while Margaret Mary found a chair on the shady side of the porch to sit for a few hours. The others watched as Buster knelt, shy as a suitor, to untie and remove her worn old shoe.

"That boy is thin as a willow switch," observed Mabel May, speaking quietly to Florrie. "I bet he could take his bath in a drain pipe."

"He sure could," added Florrie. "But that boy Buster would wiggle and jiggle so much he'd bump the itsy bitsy spider right outa her own home."

The women laughed out loud as he danced jubilantly toward the barn, holding his friend's shoe aloft in two large hands. "That Buster is a real happy boy!" exclaimed Florrie. Her brown cheeks glowed and her good eye gleamed with excitement.

Three hogs in the holding pen near the barn acted as if they shared Buster and Florrie's happiness. As the lanky farmhand danced past, they stood on their hind legs, hooked their front feet over the rail and squealed in unison.

# TWENTY

ಚಿಞ

After shyly accepting thanks from the women for fixing Margaret Mary's shoe, Buster accepted their invitation to make a fourth at Parcheesi. He scrubbed up after work to spend evenings in their company, shaking dice in a cup and moving colored markers around the board. Since the women's sitting room was off limits to men, the foursome met on the porch to play Parcheesi when the weather was fair.

Buster was the first to make up nicknames. He called the elders Fudge and Divinity when the foursome began reminiscing about making homemade candy. Nobody could afford sugar during these hard times but they liked to remember the days when holidays were celebrated with sweets. He tested it in a joking way and relaxed when Margaret Mary and Mabel May acted tickled to be called Divinity and Fudge. Others soon picked it up and candy nicknames began to catch on around the Manor House. Folks called each other Licorice Stick, Butterfingers or Snickers. Some inmates remained bigoted and standoffish but many used playful nicknames. Hard racial stereotypes began to soften like Hershey bars in the sun.

Margaret Mary was the first to notice spots of affection coloring Buster's cheeks when he said Florrie's name, and the way his ears reddened whenever he heard her lyrical voice speaking his.

And Mabel May was the first to announce it. "You two are falling in love!" And so they were, despite being of two different races.

+++

Buster asked Florrie to come to the barn alone, to meet him after work. As she approached there he was waiting, his hair gleaming gold in the lemony light. Margaret Mary heard these details the next day from Mabel May, who may have exaggerated what Florrie told her. After all, both women had romantic hearts and they were so hungry for sweetheart stories that nobody could blame them for spicing up some of the details.

As Mabel May told it, the girl had love-struck eyes when she saw Buster's hair shining with a light all its own. His chest hair shimmered, too, Florrie said, making her want to reach inside his work shirt and tangle her fingers in it. In fact, she admitted wanting to pull off his faded blue shirt, the denim that exactly matched his eyes, to yank it right off his back. When she heard this, Margaret Mary felt a pang of pure desire that caused her insides to lurch. Slender young Florrie showed the way she'd moved toward him, sinuously, conscious that he was watching. Mabel May tried to depict all this to Divinity, though her body was bulkier.

That afternoon Buster confided to Margaret Mary what had happened the day before. He said it'd made him dizzy, the light, quick way Florrie moved toward him. He said he couldn't take his eyes off her, the outline of her curves beneath the folds of her dress. She had come to him wearing a pretty sundress that glowed against her dark skin, He stuttered as he tried to say "lemon drops, the color of lemon drops." Her dress had what Florrie called a sweetheart neckline. "Sweetheart. Here comes my sweetheart," he'd stammered. The vision of it choked up his voice, and caught in Margaret Mary's throat, too.

"When Buster said her name, his voice came out all rough and desperate," Divinity later told Fudge. This was such a delicious story, and each had heard parts of it. What better way to spend a bright afternoon than comparing notes on what their young friends had told them, and what they'd left out. Margaret Mary was happy that Buster trusted her enough to describe his romantic encounter with Florrie and give more details when she asked. He'd described pulling her into the dim shadows of the barn, where the fragrance of newly baled hay filled the air with sweetness. He'd looked enchanted as he told how they'd discovered their mutual attraction. He showed how he'd traced the line of Florrie's collarbone with one finger then wrapped his long freckled arms around her dark body.

She'd been nervous at first, he said, and had pulled away. He closed his eyes when he described this part to Divinity and she did the same as she told Fudge, arranging her face to show a young man's anguish. Then after a while she didn't pull away. Buster showed how Florrie had set her two hands at his waist and strained upward to meet him. He'd kissed her then, kissed her eyelids, her ears, her throat. They'd both told this part the same way, and blushed in the telling. He'd kissed the curve where her neck met her shoulder. It gave her a damp, fluttery feeling, Florrie told Mabel May. Oh, my, I really shouldn't, she'd murmured, until his mouth touched hers. Then she couldn't think any more. Buster's kisses tasted like raisins, she said. That surprised her, and made her hungry for more. Fudge tried to describe it, how the girl's cheeks had glowed, how her blush brought out the reddish undertone of her walnut skin.

They'd not been kissing for very long, at least not like this. Fudge and Divinity both knew this to be true because they'd been watching. The young people had started with breezy pecks on the cheek after Parcheesi games, when they were pretending to be just friends. Now it sounded like more parts were getting involved. Lips, tongues, open mouths. Tightening arms. Pressing bodies.

Hearing their account of what had happened in private stirred powerful longings at the roots of young and old alike. All four - the young lovers and the older listeners - were having some sensational new feelings.

As Florrie told it, they'd been startled out of their kissing when a flurry of barn swallows suddenly swooped down. There stood Jericho Taylor in the open barn door, hefty black arms crossed over his chest. Mabel May demonstrated how the cobbler looked, as mimed by Florrie. Then she showed how the girl had stood to her full height beneath the shelter of Buster's arm and looked right up into Jericho's measuring eye. The girl's posture reflected her confidence. Florrie showed how the man's lips formed a straight line and how his big head shook firmly from side to side. And she showed how her head nodded up and down, just as firmly. An airy sense of exhilaration filled Margaret Mary's chest even though she was hearing Florrie's account second-hand.

+++

The budding romance between Florrie and Buster caused more gossip than anything the Manor House had heard in ages. "Don'cha know it's against the law in this state for whites and blacks to marry," insisted Jericho. "Every last man of us will face prison time if we're part of this."

"But slavery's behind us," said Ben. "You're all free negroes now. You can't be convicted of any crime, not if the county clerk gives them a marriage license." Everyone had an opinion. Racial tensions surfaced, causing divisions among friends and arguments between strangers.

When the young couple announced that they planned to get married, Margaret Mary was all in favor. "How exciting," she said enthusiastically. "New love gives everybody a lift, even if it is between black and white."

Mabel May was adamantly opposed. "Where will they live, tell me that. You know there is no place for married people here on the Farm. And who will rent to a mixed couple, tell me that. Florrie already has enough problems without marrying a white man."

# TWENTY-ONE

॰৫৪੦

As Margaret Mary saw it, the young couple's romance was ruining her friendship with Mabel May. They had been tense with each other all week and then it got worse.

"I do not want that big bucket of lard in my knitting group," Mabel May insisted in her determined way. They were looking down the hall at Tillie, a new inmate, stuffed into a wheelchair. A white line of slip dripped below the hem of her blue cotton dress. Rolls of flesh larded her thighs and belly. The skin on her face drooped like a saggy teabag.

"I only suggested inviting Tillie to join the knitting group because she's so good with her hands," said Margaret Mary. Her voice sounded mousy. Unconvincing.

"No" said Mabel May. "No, no, no." Her strong contralto voice was made for command. She hadn't told anyone here, but her uncle started calling her The Major when she was just a little girl.

"Well, who put you in charge, anyway," snapped Margaret Mary, turning her back and stomping off. She smacked her cane against the floor with more force than usual.

+++

Later that day she discovered Mabel May and Florrie with their heads together, ignoring her. Margaret Mary had walked away, not believing it was true. They had not turned against her, they couldn't have. Her body gave all the signs of having stumbled into a crisis. There was a tingling in her chin and fingertips, shaking in her legs so severe that she had trouble walking. Her breathing was fast and shallow. Still, her mind said: *There has been some mistake. It is not true that my friends have gone sour on me.*

+++

After disagreeing about Buster & Florrie, then arguing about Tillie, it was nearly impossible for Margaret Mary and Mabel May to speak to each other. The few words they did exchange came out stiff. If their eyes met, both glanced away. In the crowded ward they moved past each other carefully. They were separated by only one cot, unoccupied at the moment. Margaret Mary knew when Mabel May wasn't sleeping by the restless way her friend kept turning over in bed.

When did this begin? Her legs jerked uncontrollably as she lay on her cot. As she went through it in her mind, she allowed herself a moment of approval there in the darkness, because it was good of her not to have said a thing about Negros sticking together. But her two friends had left her out and that hurt. It pained her each time she remembered their turned-away faces, Mabel May and Florrie hunching together with their shoulders touching. How they went quiet when she came into the room, how they sat stone-still as if she wasn't there. Then how she, Margaret Mary, had opened a window. The air inside the sitting room had struck her as stagnant, so she'd pushed the window up and stood there, leaning against the windowsill. She remembered the terrible weight of her own hips and the awful weight of her friends' silence.

Margaret Mary, who was old enough to know better, nevertheless could not stop herself from thinking that Mabel May was in the wrong for opposing the marriage of two people who were clearly meant for each other. Lying in her bed in the summer darkness - a darkness that seemed overheated by irritation - she found it necessary to go over everything again in her head, trying to sort out her confused thoughts and feelings.

+++

How long could this go on, eating meals across the table from each other but not speaking a word. It was ridiculous to arrive at the latrine at the same time, sitting in stalls so close together and separated by such thin partitions that they could smell each other's pee. It crossed Margaret Mary's mind to ask for a transfer to the other women's ward - the one across the hall - because there was a vacancy. But moving would require more energy than she had. It would also require an explanation she was not prepared to give. She felt righteous and misunderstood, but she was not ready, even now, to release Mabel May as her friend.

Tears leaked from her eyes in the dark. She sensed that in order to calm down - to find some way to mend things with Mabel May and Florrie - her body would need to become totally still. Exerting great willpower over her muscles, she made the restless jerking of her legs stop. Once she'd done that, she also found it possible to quiet her restless thoughts. *God help me,* she thought, *I have no idea what to do.*

+++

"Mabel May's face stared back at me from the mirror last night," she whispered to Bella. "Her eyes were sparking. She looked furious. She had a silver knife in her hand."

'What are you talking about?" Bella's broad forehead furrowed with concern.

"I got up in the middle of the night to go to the bathroom. When I glanced in the mirror I saw her face instead of my own. Do you think I'm going off my rocker?"

"You two still aren't getting along, are you?" Bella asked, although she knew.

"No." Margaret Mary shook her head and sighed.

"It's sad," Bella said. She patted her friend's arm. "What do you want?"

"I want to be friends again. I want things to be like they were before the fight. I want us to help Buster and Florrie get married, to work together on the wedding. And I want the newlyweds to live happily ever after."

"What do you think Mabel May wants?"

"I think she wants to make buttons out of my bones." She paused, as if startled by this idea. Bella stared, speechless. "She's treating me like a dead whale, like someone who's stinking up her beach."

"Where'd you get this idea, anyway?"

"Bad dream. The stink of rotting whale meat got into my nose last night, and the sight of Mabel May holding a silver knife woke me up."

"How awful," said Bella.

"She's been glaring at me since I told everyone how excited I am about Buster and Florrie getting married. She hates the idea, and now she hates me, too."

"Well, I like you," said Bella, "and I like that blue sweater on you. Did I ever tell you about my favorite Italian sweater?" She was trying to change the subject. "Aunt Maria knitted it, with buttons made of bone. They last forever," started Bella.

Margaret Mary's scowl cut her off. "My point exactly," she snapped.

# TWENTY-TWO

☙☙

Buster and Florrie would marry on August 26, the very day she had wed George. This news put Margaret Mary in a tizzy. She'd been on the porch knitting when Buster came by. He had no idea, of course, that August 26 was her wedding anniversary. Before she could get her thoughts together to tell him, Buster stunned her with another bombshell. He wanted her to be his matron of honor. One of two. Florrie had asked Mabel May to be the other. Yes, they knew of the upset. And yes, they trusted Divinity and Fudge to make up.

After Buster left she picked up her needles again and tried to knit her way through the wild thicket of thoughts and feelings that tangled in heart and mind. She was knitting navy-blue leg warmers for Irma Bates in the sick ward. Odd that Irma had the chill-blains at the height of summer. The air was warm, but Margaret Mary found herself shivering. *Maybe I'm getting the chill-blains, too.*

+++

Later, she told Bella about the wedding that was to come and the one she remembered from forty-seven years ago. Talking to a friend helped. She could sort out her tangled feelings better with someone there to listen.

"It was a late summer wedding," she said, "in 1889. I wore an ivory dress of fine cotton. My mother trimmed it with lace from her own wedding dress. I'd never felt so pretty before, or since. Now I just feel matronly," she grumbled, glancing down at her wide lap, "but I guess that's how a matron of honor is supposed to feel."

"Did you carry flowers at your wedding?" asked Bella.

"I did. I carried a beautiful bouquet of roses. Bride's Dream, they were called." She heaved a big, bosomy sigh. Her eyes went dreamy in remembrance.

"I don't know Bride's Dream. What were they like, your roses?" nudged Bella.

"Pink, a pale satiny pink," she said, "and so fragrant." A pink tinge colored her face. Bella wondered if the bouquet was the same color as her friend's cheeks but decided not to ask.

"And your groom?" she asked.

"George was the handsomest groom you ever did see," she said. "We were married in front of my mother's fireplace. Neither of us could take our eyes off his reflection in the mirror above the mantel. I loved the way he smoothed his hair with two damp fingertips. Even his fingernails gleamed. When I saw how George caressed his cuticles, I knew he'd soon be touching me that way."

"And did he?"

"Yes, for a while."

+++

The matrons of honor made up, as Buster and Florrie knew they would. It made things all right again when she learned why Mabel May and Florrie had their heads together that day. The girl was using every ounce of persuasion she had to convince the stubborn woman to support their marriage across black and white lines.

Women in the knitting group plundered their trunks for traditional items to give the bride. Something old, something new, something borrowed and something blue. Nurse Bessie's pastor conducted the ceremony beneath an apple tree in the orchard. Two of Florrie's sisters stood up with her. Margaret Mary and Mabel May stood up with Buster. Guests dabbed hankies dabbed at their eyes when the bride said "I do." Florrie looked like a sunbeam gazing up into her groom's face. Nobody laughed when he stammered his vows. The gospel choir sang *How Great Thou Art.*" A hurricane of happy honeybees led the wedding procession.

It was an exciting week, the most romantic in the memory of most inmates. Later, the knitting group collected bits of news from each other. As needles flashed, each knitter reported what she'd heard before, during and after the wedding.

"Did you know the Farm Manager let them spend their wedding night in the loft of the barn?" Bella got this on good authority from one of the farmhands.

"And that Jericho stood guard through the night?"

"Whatever for?" asked Alma in her tiny voice.

"To keep watch in case the sheriff came to arrest them." Mabel May had a nervous flutter in her voice.

"He also kept watch so none of those rowdy farmhands could sneak into the barn and pester them," announced Margaret Mary. Her tone was firm as granite. "Jericho didn't want the men to do what was called a shivaree in the olden days so he stood guard but from a discreet distance." Everyone nodded, glad that the big cobbler had gone from opposing their union to sheltering the newlyweds. The women agreed he'd done a good deed, protecting Buster and Florrie from who-knows-what-kind of nonsense.

"Did you hear Florrie's sister works at a bakery in Gresham?" asked Mabel May. She had the most up-to-date news about the bride. "There's a furnished room above the bakery and they can live there." Pride puffed out her chest, as though Fudge herself had arranged this fine housing for the young couple.

"Any chance Florrie can get work as a baker's helper?" asked Alma.

"I hope so," murmured Margaret Mary. "I've been worrying how they'll get by."

"Everybody needs shoe repair these days," declared Bella. "I'm praying to Saint Martin de Porres to help get Buster a job."

The women went quiet. In her mind's eye, Margaret Mary could see her lanky friend bent over a cobbler's bench, replacing a worn sole.

"And wasn't that a sight," exclaimed Mabel May, "when Florrie and Buster drove away in the back of that fancy red roadster, waving over their shoulders."

"Lily White is more than a physical therapist," said Margaret Mary. "In my opinion, she is a miracle worker, getting her friend to drive them to Gresham."

"And wasn't that grand, all of us lined up on the porch, waving and waving until they were out of sight," sighed Mabel May.

"How do you suppose Lily White knew they needed a ride to Gresham, anyway?" asked Alma. Nobody claimed to know. If someone did, she kept quiet about it.

+++

"Have you thought any more about Tillie?" asked Margaret Mary. It had been a month since the wedding and the friends were back on good terms.

"What about her?"

"About inviting her into our knitting group."

They gazed in Tillie's direction as she sat in her wheelchair at the end of the hall. Creases marked her face and arms, but it was her hair that caused the most gossip around the Manor House. It may once have been red but was now a dirty manure color with wide streaks of white. They watched as she grasped her oddly striped hair in both hands and pulled, scowling and shaking her jowls from side to side.

"Why is she always yanking on her hair that way?" Mabel May challenged.

"Maybe she pulls her hair when things aren't going right, when she doesn't know what else to do." Margaret Mary stopped. "Oh, my goodness. I sounded just like my Aunt Virginia right then," she said. "Almost motherly."

"Well, Tillie certainly is not the motherly type," snapped Mabel May. "She is one of those vinegary type people. I do not want some big fat woman with a sharp tongue sitting and knitting next to me."

"Speaking of tongues," Margaret Mary interrupted, looking sideways at her friend, "I know someone who has mouth full of brass tacks her own self. That tongue of yours would be a match for Tillie's any day."

Mabel May's eyes and mouth stood wide open.

Margaret Mary eased her sharp words with a grin. "Isn't that right, Fudge?"

"Well." A matching grin stole over Mabel May's face. "I suppose you may be right. Divinity."

"So, I'll say it again. I bet they'll have a baby before long. We need some skilled knitters if we're to outfit a new little child. And Tillie is a whiz with her hands."

Mabel May stared down the hall at the odd woman, at the rolls of flesh spilling over the edges of her wheelchair. "She sure looks untidy," she mused.

"That woman is unhappy, Fudge. You would be, too, if nobody paid any attention to you. She wouldn't look so bad if people treated her half-way nice." Her voice was firm, and so was her gaze. "But that's enough. I've said my piece."

She waited for her friend to say something. Instead, Mabel May strode down the hall, footsteps as clipped as her manner of speech. *For a stout woman, she sure has a jerky way of stepping,* thought Margaret Mary.

"Hello, there. How are you doing this fine day?"

The heavy, lopsided woman looked up in surprise.

"I guess I'm doing as well as can be expected, for someone in my condition."

Margaret Mary listened as they passed the time of day. *Why,* she thought, *Tillie's voice is so lovely, sharp and sweet together. It has the ache of life in it and the joy of heaven, both at the same time. If a stick of peppermint could talk, that's just the way it would sound.*

# TWENTY-THREE

### ⳽

"Do you know what I heard today! You'll never guess," Bella whispered to Margaret Mary. They were standing beside the window watching torrents of rain pour off the roof. "I got to tell you now, while nobody else is around," Bella went on in an urgent voice. "It's a terrible secret."

"Whose secret? Yours?"

"No, Jasper's. That tall young man who walks like a dancing girl."

"Who? Oh, I know the one you mean..."

"You've seen him around, very big and manly looking. But his voice is so high-pitched it always makes me look around to see if someone else is talking."

"So, where did you hear this terrible secret?"

"Down in the basement. I was looking around for a place to set up my lace-making frame. That rude Lex was getting his hair cut, telling Patrick the barber all about Jasper. They were so busy gossiping, they didn't notice me."

"What were they gossiping about?"

"What happened a few years ago at the YMCA." Bella's voice dropped to a whisper. "What happened that got those fellows arrested. Jasper was one of them. And what happened in jail. Lex was doing time in county jail. It's almost too awful to talk about."

"Oh, I remember that scandal," said Margaret Mary. "It was about some hanky-panky between men at the downtown Y in Portland, right?"

"Yes," hissed Bella," it was so scandalous it made the headlines. After they got those girly men out of the YMCA and into county jail, more dirty stuff went on. What was the sheriff thinking, putting queer men in the same cell."

"I remember Father McCarthy preaching against that, after the newspaper printed such raw stuff on the front page."

"But that's not the worst of it." Bella paused, turning her gaze out the window. Piles of black clouds lurked along the horizon and a stiff wind carried small branches along the ground.

Margaret Mary tugged at her friend's sleeve. "Then what happened?"

"Patrick asked Lex that same question. I had to listen with all my might, because Lex lowered his voice. It sounded like he said the judge sentenced Jasper to prison but his lawyer got him off."

"How do you mean?"

"Here's the terrible part. Lex boomed this out like thunder. The judge said that under the state law he could give Jasper and his buddy a choice. They could either be sentenced to Oregon State Prison for the rest of their lives. Or." Bella swallowed and looked behind her to make sure nobody was within hearing distance. "Or, the judge would let them go free." Her voice failed and she swallowed again.

"Go free?"

"Only if they agreed to be" she lowered her voice and whispered "castrated."

"Oh, my goodness." Margaret Mary placed both hands over her heart.

"Yes." Bella paused dramatically with both eyebrows high. "And we know he's not in prison."

"Mercy sakes. I've heard George and his friends talk about the awful things that convicts do to each other in prison, especially to girly men. Someone who walks and talks like Jasper could never survive behind bars."

"So that means…"

"Young Jasper has been castrated."

"Lord, have mercy."

"What do we do with his terrible secret?"

"God only knows."

+++

"That's a lovely pink rosary," she blurted, trying to catch Jasper's attention before he got away. Men were only permitted in the second-floor women's sitting room during Mass when a visiting priest was presiding. The liturgy had just ended. Margaret Mary spotted the graceful young man trying to make his exit. People greeting Father Finnegan blocked the doorway. Jasper looked edgy, nervous.

"I'm Margaret Mary Wright," she said, "and you are?"

He mumbled something, maybe Jasper Carroll.

"My rosary was a gift from the Mother Superior," she said hastily, lifting her beads high to catch his eye. *I hope this boy had a strict Catholic mother. Good manners may be the only thing keeping him from racing away.*

"Mother Superior gave me these beads because I started out to be a nun when I was your age." *I'm talking too fast*, she thought, spurting on.

"Did you ever think about being a priest?"

"A priest?" Jasper's face flushed.

She caught his hand and tugged him toward a couch. As soon as they sat, she thrust her beads into one of Jasper's big hands. He held his own rosary in the other.

"Where did you get those pretty pink rosary beads?"

"Father Valdico gave them to me a few years ago. 'To my favorite altar boy,' he said. He gave me other things, too.…"

"Other things?"

"Wine. And other stuff..."

Jasper's face was bright red now. She saw confusion in his eyes. He quickly looked down at his lap. Time to change the subject.

"Mother Superior taught me that the rosary is a sacred object. And my dear old Scottish grandmother called the rosary her spiritual treasury. Granny told me the beads helped her focus on the Blessed Virgin instead of on herself."

Jasper tossed pink beads lightly from one hand to the other. Both his eyes were shut tight.

"What did Father Valdico teach you about the rosary?" She spoke insistently, emphasizing the word you.

"He told me the rosary is a powerful weapon," the young man replied in his odd, high-pitched voice. "He said it's stronger than a Gatling gun if you point it at your enemies."

Margaret Mary gulped at the violence of this comparison but Jasper didn't notice her reaction. He seemed to be conversing with his eyes closed.

"Father Valdico said that if you're holding the rosary when you die, it brings the Blessed Virgin right to your side. She'll take you straight to heaven."

+++

Margaret Mary couldn't get Jasper off her mind. She couldn't imagine what the poor boy must be suffering. To get him out of her thoughts, she stared across Halsey Street and concentrated on the dull metal railroad tracks glinting in the winter light. She tried following the line east in her imagination. *Those great stretches of metal link me to George,* she mused. *Maybe Albert, too, if he passed here on his way to God knows where.*

Loud hoots and a cacophony of catcalls interrupted her reverie. Margaret Mary stood up and looked over the porch railing to find out what was going on. Down near the pool hall a bunch of skinny men crowded around two who were throwing knives. *I bet they're playing mumblety-peg,* she thought, watching bristly-chinned guys tossing jackknives in the air. When blades landed point-down close to the shoes of an opponent, the crowd cheered. When knives went astray, they booed.

+++

That evening she described to Ben and Bella what happened next. "Jasper, that big sugar bear, stood at the edge of the crowd. Lex and Cox turned and spat on him. Half a dozen men copied the roughnecks. Some aimed for his face and some for his feet."

"What did you do?" asked Ben.

"At first I was too shocked to do anything. Then something came over me and I called out I'm watching you.

"Good choice," murmured Ben. "Then what?"

"Some in the crowd turned and looked up toward me, standing above them on the porch. I must have startled a few of the men enough to dry up their spit but Lex and Cox spat at Jasper again. So I said it again, yelling as loud as I could. I AM STILL WATCHING YOU!"

"Wow," said Bella, eyes wide open. "I'm impressed."

"Jasper looked at Cox, stared him right in the eye, then glared at Lex. He pulled out his handkerchief and wiped off his face. Then he turned and walked away without a word. And just then, the very moment Jasper turned his back, the sky opened up and soaked us."

"Like in the Bible," said Bella in a reverent tone. She drew a quick breath and added, "Are they plotting to harm him, do you think? Or kill him?"

"Those no-gooders have something against Jews and homos," said Ben. He spoke in a slow, deliberate way. "I've heard too much violent talk from those two. Lex and Cox may be true Commies or maybe they're just big-talking bullies. Want to help me find out?"

"I'm not brave enough to talk to those men directly," said Margaret Mary. "Are you?"

"Getting braver the more I hear how they treat men like Jasper," said Ben. His expression was alert, yet courteous. "It gives me courage, listening to President Roosevelt in those fireside chats of his."

"Yes," grinned Margaret Mary. She lowered the pitch of her voice to imitate Franklin Delano Roosevelt. "My friends, says our President - like he knows how we feel - my fellow Americans, the only thing we have to fear is fear itself.'"

It felt good to laugh. After the hilarity died down, Bella said "That makes me feel a little braver, too."

"Roosevelt may not have it all figured out like the Reds say they do," added Ben, "but he's not afraid to make some bold moves. Our President is taking big risks to get people back to work, to get the economy moving again. I figure it's time for us to take a few risks here. For the good of the order."

"You make me feel patriotic," said Margaret Mary. She burst into song and Ben joined in. Bella didn't know the words to The Star Spangled Banner but the meaning was clear in their triumphant finale.

"In the laaand of the FREEEEEE,

"And the home of the BRRAAAAVE!"

# TWENTY-FOUR

ଓଆ

"That flu epidemic sure knocked the wind out of everyone," she told Ben later. "I about wore myself out holding basins under chins and wiping foreheads."

"Lily White told me you kept calm through it all, sitting with patients and giving a bit of comfort," he replied. "What was that like for you?"

"Sitting through the night with Molly Kelly, that was a trial all right. She was such a troubled soul, and a frightening sight with her crazed face and cracked lips. Nurse Rachel warned me about Molly's torments, but said she figured I was the strong enough to stay close even if the terrors came upon the poor woman."

"And were you?" asked Ben. The corners of his mouth crinkled with affection.

"Not in the beginning. Her first wail scared the wits out of me, sounded like a fox caught by an eagle. She was shrieking something about torn knickers and bloody thighs. I didn't understand all of it, just enough to know she'd gone through something awful.

"'Grab a garden rake' she told me, grabbing tight to my hand. 'I've got hold of an ax. Keep quiet now,' she ordered me, so we can sneak up and kill him.'"

"Kill who?"

"The one who raped her, I figured. Molly's tremors got so bad I feared her teeth would come loose. She looked weak but those bony claws of hers had a death grip on me. She shrieked whenever I tried to pry loose. That poor woman held onto me for dear life until she went unconscious. That was a blessed relief for both of us."

"Too bad the poor soul had to die," he said, "but it must have been her time."

"I prayed to keep Molly Kelly here on earth until Mother Mary herself started talking to me. 'You may let go now, dear one,' the Holy Mother said in that sweet firm voice of hers. 'It is time for me to take my dear daughter home to our Heavenly Father.' Now if that wasn't the Blessed Virgin herself I don't know who it could have been."

Ben simply tilted his head. He had no idea what to say to that. She took a deep breath and went on.

"After reporting Molly's death I dropped into bed like a limb breaking off an oak. Exhausted but I still couldn't sleep. I kept sensing something going on above my head."

"Above your head?" Ben sounded puzzled.

"I know, it sounds odd but I've got the Lord Jesus over my bed. On his cross, you know. Sister Kathleen gave me that crucifix before I was married, so I've taken Jesus everywhere I've ever lived. But on the night Molly Kelly died, something about him seemed different."

"Different, how?"

"More alive somehow. As if Jesus was staying awake to look after me. I told Jesus I was grateful he was there keeping watch because my head felt awful hot and achy. What if Molly's flu germs were getting hold of me? My mouth was dry as popcorn. I told our Lord I didn't have the pep to get up and fetch some water."

Ben kept his eyes on her face as she described fretting and tossing under the covers.

PART TWO : MARGARET MARY THE JOURNEY | 1935 - 37

Suddenly Margaret Mary heaved herself to her feet and abruptly left the room. *She left without so much as a word,* he thought. *I've never known her to be rude. Wonder what's going on.*

As he sat alone Ben recalled a lioness he'd once watched at the Portland Zoo, pacing back and forth in a too-small cage.

+++

*I've got to talk about all this.* She knew that. *But how can I possibly tell what happened without being thought mad?*

*What did happen?* She tried to reason it out, imagining how Ben would ask questions in that light way of his. *He'll help me sort this out if I can get up the gumption to tell him. And if Ben thinks I've gone off my rocker, then maybe I have.*

She practiced how to tell her unbelievable experience in a believable way. *I'll tell him I had a fever and a queasy stomach, like I was in a rowboat. I was feeling dauncey, afraid I was about to tip out and sink. That's when Our Lord himself leaned down from his cross and bent his face close to mine.*

"Did he say anything?" She imagined what Ben would ask.

*Yes.* Her face flushed at the memory. *Yes, He did.*

Margaret Mary practiced telling the truth of it in her own mind. *His feet were still nailed to the cross, but not his hands. Jesus bent forward from the waist and peered right into my face. He said "I look as stiff as you feel." I was so flabbergasted I just stared up at him and couldn't say a word. Then Jesus said "Soon you will feel better. Now rest in peace."*

This last part of the memory seemed most realistic, although she wondered about those last words. She had seen R.I.P engraved on tombstones. *When Jesus said Rest in Peace did he mean it as a benediction? Or was he warning me that I was about to die in my sleep? But I didn't die that night, did I? In fact, I slept like a newborn once I stopped fretting, once I could trust Jesus to be with me no matter what happened.*

For days, Margaret Mary rehearsed what she would say to Ben. He was the only one she could trust with this, but she felt skittish, couldn't get up the nerve to go downstairs to his watch-repair shop.

"Then what?" She kept practicing how to describe her indescribable experience. Ben used short, simple words so she tried to do that. *I'll tell him that once the rocking-boat motion stopped, I couldn't have moved if the house caught fire. I'll say that eventually I went back to sleep. I did feel better when I woke up. Next morning Jesus was back in his usual place on the cross above my bed and the whole thing seemed like some kind of fever dream.*

+++

She was greatly relieved when Ben stepped onto the porch a few days later. It was a windy afternoon. She had just settled into her favorite chair, wrapped in a gray and yellow striped woolen afghan. Margaret Mary was so grateful to see him that she barely said hello before blurting "Can I tell you about my fever dream?" He listened attentively as she poured out the whole story, the way she had rehearsed it.

"If it was a dream, how are you feeling about it now?"

She was suddenly flooded with affection for this small, sweet man. She covered her confusion by pulling the afghan to her chin, warding off the bitter wind.

"What reaction did you have that night?" He asked it differently the second time.

"What reaction did I have?" Repeating Ben's question helped corral the thoughts jumping around in her head like fleas on a dog.

"It was such a strange experience that not even I can believe it," she answered, closing her eyes. *How did I feel when Jesus leaned down from his cross and put his cool hand on my cheek?*

"I felt his holy hand right here." She lightly rested her fingertips against her left cheek.

"Did Jesus touch you with the tips of his fingers?" Ben probed.

"No...."

She remembered more.

"No." She spoke with more assurance.

"No, he touched me like this."

She extended her fingers and placed the flat of her left palm firmly against the left side of her face. "He didn't push. His touch was gentle but firm. Then he did this." Margaret Mary raised her right hand and rested it across the length of her forehead.

"Jesus has bigger hands than mine," she said, glancing down at her lap. "And yours," she added with an appreciative glance at Ben's slender fingers.

"Did he say anything else?"

Ben's expression was filled with such tender care that it made her weep. She lifted a corner of the afghan to catch her tears.

Both moved at the same time. Ben scooted closer and Margaret Mary leaned forward. When her head touched his heart they rested there, each comforted by the warmth of the other.

# TWENTY-FIVE

◦₃₈◦

"Where have you been lately?" Ben asked. "I've missed our evening walks."

Poor Farm rules kept the genders separated. Men ate in the mess hall on the main floor and women dined on the second floor. They had taken to meeting on the porch when the weather allowed and strolling the grounds together.

"I've needed quiet time lately," she replied. "Got a lot to think about..." She didn't know how to finish the sentence so she let her words trail off.

"Thinking about anything in particular?" Ben replied in his milk-mild way.

She nodded, gazing at him. Smallpox scars marked Ben's face. At first, she'd ignored the curdled texture of his complexion but had gradually grown accustomed to it. The low angle of evening light cast long shadows on his features, giving the impression of a mysterious moonscape rather than the familiar face of a friend.

*Who is this man?* she wondered, not for the first time. *What secrets are hiding in the crevices of his face? How did he become so thoughtful, so tender? There is more to Benjamin Borden than I will ever know.*

He reached for her hand and Margaret Mary let him twine his string-bean fingers between her carrot-plump ones. They walked for a while in silence. He glanced at her face and saw something there that prompted him to remain still.

"It's about Molly Kelly." Her voice was small. She sounded tentative, like a little girl. Ben waited for his friend to go on.

"I don't know what happened to her...."

"You told me about sitting with Molly her last night on earth, that she held tight to your hand when she died. Is that what you mean?"

"No. Something terrible happened to her when she was a girl. It's something too awful to talk about. But I keep imagining it anyway..."

"How can I help?"

"I don't know where they took her body. There's no cemetery here. There's no place I can go to pray for Molly's soul, no place to put flowers..."

Her voice caught. She didn't know it yet but deep in her soul, Margaret Mary wanted a way to mourn with her friends, a place to remember those they had lost.

Ben saw her body crumple and realized she needed to sit down. He swiftly removed his jacket and laid it across a boulder near the base of a tree. Taking Margaret Mary's hand, he tugged her gently and held her arm as she settled her generous bulk onto the rock. Ben lowered himself onto stringy haunches, heard both knees pop, and hunkered at his friend's eye level.

"How about dedicating this stone to Molly's memory," he proposed.

Wordlessly she pondered this, then nodded. She held out her hands. Ben rose to his feet and pulled her up. She gestured toward a small patch of pink flowers growing near a fence post. He hummed quietly as she bent to pick a handful of sweet-pea blossoms. She needed to bring a bit of beauty to Molly's memorial. She laid the fragrant pink blooms beside the stone, bowed her head and fingered the rosary beads looped around her left wrist. "Hail Mary, full of grace," she whispered. Ben waited in his tranquil way until her lips stopped moving.

"What was that prayer?" he inquired. Born and bred Baptist, Ben found Margaret Mary's religious rituals both strange and fascinating. "The Sorrowful Mysteries," she replied. "The sad part of the Holy Rosary reminds me of Jesus in the Garden of Gethsemane." Margaret Mary glanced up to see if he was following this.

Ben's smile shone briefly, then ducked back inside as if uncertain of the weather.

"Jesus sweated blood as he faced the torture ahead. Then he surrendered to his Heavenly Father. Not my will but thine be done."

Ben cocked his head to one side as if he was trying to figure something out. It was hard to guess what he thought, or didn't. She paused, searching for the best way to explain.

"I pray for Molly's soul," she plunged on, "for her eternal peace. Each bead," she went on, holding her Rosary up to catch the long rays of western light, "reminds me of the different ways Jesus suffered at the end."

She glanced up and saw Ben's gaze lit with interest. His eyes had turned the color of fog just as the sun begins to shine through. "Go on," he said with a small smile.

"This bead stands for when Jesus was whipped. This one is how awful it feels to be mocked. This bead represents the pain of having thorns on your head. The next ones follow him up the hill to Calvary, marking each time he fell beneath the weight of the cross."

"What do your rosary beads have to do with Molly Kelly?" His tone was curt.

*Ben cannot abide an unasked question,* she thought. She eyed him with disapproval, impatient at being interrupted.

"My beads remind me what its like to be abandoned and betrayed!" She replied so forcefully that Margaret Mary sounded to herself just like Mother Superior at the convent where she'd stayed for a short time. That tongue-lashing still stung. Her ears warmed with the memory. Her facial skin remembered too, flushing hot at the shame she had felt in leaving the novitiate. At the time she had stammered and blushed, trying to describe the wonder of falling in love with George Wright and accepting his marriage proposal. Mother Superior had mocked her for "leaving the holy work of The Church to become a silly housewife." But she didn't tell Ben any of this.

"This is how I pray," she said simply, giving a little shake of the head to bring her focus back to the spring evening. "This is hard to explain, but I was taught it is better to confess my sins than to harden my heart. I pray for people who suffer and die. I pray to the Blessed Virgin to help Molly forgive the man who hurt her, to forgive the people who let her down. I pray that the love and mercy of Jesus will redeem her from sin. I just want Molly's soul to be at peace...." Her words trailed off.

The pair sat for a while in silence.

"What do you think happened to Molly's soul after she died?" He sounded melancholy.

*Purgatory, that's what,* she thought. *Purgatory, where purging fire burns sin from the soul. Where souls are purified by punishment. But I have no idea how to explain the Church's teaching so a Baptist will understand.*

"You told me how you tended to Molly when she was dying, how you kept her company that last night..." Ben's plaintive voice trailed off.

Margaret Mary's brow was furrowed like the plowed field beyond the fence. As the newly turned soil awaited its seed, Ben awaited understanding from his Roman Catholic friend.

"What do I think happened to Molly's soul?" She paused to gather her thoughts. She'd developed a habit of repeating his questions and Ben found this endearing. He respected her for taking all the time she needed. Margaret Mary's answers were worth waiting for.

"The priest says that all of us are sinners. He says that we go to purgatory first..."

"But what do YOU say?"

She looked up, startled by his urgency.

"I have a spiritual interest in this," he said. "Baptists preach fire and brimstone but that vision of hell doesn't set well with me. Why would a good God punish his own creatures with eternal damnation? I need to know what YOU think." He peered at her insistently.

"The priest is the one I go to for help..." she stammered in a quavery voice.

Ben shook his head as if pestered by flies. "That's not what I want to hear," he blurted. "I'm not interested in what some priest thinks. You're a smart woman. Tell me what you ..."

"Aren't you the one always quoting Isaiah to me?!"

Her sharpness hurt Ben's feelings. She could tell. She softened her tone. "In quietness and trust is my strength, or so you keep telling me."

"What does Isaiah have to do with this? I'm not following your logic, woman."

"Calm down, Ben. Catholics have our saints and Baptists have your prophets, right? We both need all the wisdom we can get before we wind up in a pauper's grave like Molly. So, let's make a deal. Next time we try to figure out what happens to souls after death, let's get our favorite dead men into the conversation."

"Okay." He was tentative, still stinging from her rebuttal but willing to consider her suggestion.

She flapped one hand in the direction of a far-distant cemetery then extended it toward Ben. He rose and gave a tug to help her up. The effort took both hands and a big grunt.

"I'm grateful you are my friend," she murmured, tucking one hand under his arm. They strolled in companionable silence, each thinking their own thoughts, through lilac twilight toward narrow cots in two wings of the Manor House.

# TWENTY-SIX

### ✧

Early in their marriage, before the boys were born, George taught her to play poker. Half a century had passed and she didn't remember many of the rules, but poker was on her mind. *I'm going to die anyway,* she thought, *we all are. Meanwhile, this is the hand I've been dealt.* In her mind's eye, she peered at her cards, wondering how to play a hand like this.

| | |
|---|---|
| Queen of hearts. | Twice broken, now mending. |
| Ten of clubs. | Albert's acts of violence, at least ten. The times she knew about anyway. |
| Eight of spades. | Buried cats, dogs and canaries. |
| Jack of hearts. | Her faith, still strong. |
| Queen of diamonds. | Old love and new. |

+++

On restless nights when she couldn't sleep, Margaret Mary had taken to slipping a coat over her nightgown and sitting on the porch. Lately she'd been troubling over the dilemma of strangers, questioning her old ideas. *A stranger is simply someone I've not met.* She tried on this idea. *Someone whose name I don't know* yet. *But how can I tell who's dangerous? Are some strangers safer than others?*

Gazing at the moon settled her. She could not explain to herself, let alone anyone else, why sitting alone under the night sky soothed her soul. A faithful Catholic, she shuddered at the thought of confessing this odd habit to her priest. *Father Finnegan would think I'm worshipping some sky god. He'd tell me to say twenty Hail Marys and get back to my prayers,* she figured. *It's hard, being so unsure. Are there different rules for Catholics and Protestants? For rich people and poor people?* Clouds moved across the face of the moon but she stayed put, content in the quiet company of the stars. *We all start out in this Manor House as strangers,* she mused. *It's how we treat each other, that's what matters.*

She heard the whistle - the same three notes repeated over and over - before she saw the whistler. Margaret Mary smelled the whiskey before she spotted the drinker. Suddenly aware of her pale skin, she moved beneath the shadows of the eaves as a thick-limbed Negro man on a crutch lurched up the steps of the Manor House. One black eye shone in the light of the waning moon. The other eye was missing, the hole thickened with ugly scars branching across his face. *What on earth has happened to this man?*

The drunk crashed against the doorjamb and wavered. He was no longer whistling. He steadied himself with one hand against the wall before moving inside.

Without pausing to think about it, she followed. She could not have given a reason if asked why she was doing this. She kept a few steps back as he hobbled down the hall and pushed into the men's ward. As the door swung open she heard loud waves of snoring.

*Glad I'm not sleeping in there,* she thought. *I've not heard such loud snorts since George left.* As she made her way upstairs

PART TWO : MARGARET MARY THE JOURNEY | 1935 - 37

to the women's ward she noticed that memories of George didn't hurt so much. *And I don't have terrible dreams now that he's not riding the rails. I'm relieved my brother's family took him in.*

As she settled under the quilt her heart lifted in praise. *Thank you, Mother Mary, for bringing me here, for helping me get well again. Thank you for keeping George safe in Montana. And please look after that poor soul with the one eye. His face shows a world of hurt.*

+++

"This has turned out to be a good place after all," Margaret Mary said, addressing a small group of women at the edge of the cedar grove. They sat in the shade, hands busy knitting.

"I never imagined finding friends like you-all here," added Alma in her baby voice. Five heads nodded in agreement.

"The Manor House looks so stately from this distance," remarked Betty. Six heads turned to admire their adopted home.

"Who's that man standing there looking at us?" asked Mabel May. It came out more of a growl than a whisper. Her voice sounded like a lumberjack when she got nervous.

"Do you see that Negro man watching us?" They did, but nobody spoke. "See him? That man in raggedy clothes with the crutch?"

Margaret Mary realized this was the man she'd seen stumbling drunk three nights ago.

"Why's that man standing there looking at us for?" Mabel May's tone was insistent.

Margaret Mary almost blurted "Because he envies us being friends," then quickly caught her tongue. *Where did that come from?*

"Hmmmmmmm," she said slowly, pausing her words while thinking fast. "Maybe he's looking at us because he's new here

143

and doesn't know anybody." Her hand lifted of its own accord and beckoned the shabby man to come closer. Her friends inhaled in unison, and Mabel May started to protest but simmered down as he approached.

Meager and hard of frame, he leaned on a crutch to take the weight off his right foot. They could see he was broad-handed with muscled arms. His nose was blunt and his mouth was lipless. Pinkish-brownish scars jagged across the right side of his face from mouth to ear, from hairline to jawline. They gulped at the sight of the man's scarred face and sightless eye.

"Good afternoon, ladies. I'm new here at the farm. Let me introduce myself. My name is Jack Smith."

The chocolatey flow of his voice relaxed the nervous women. He paused for a beat then added "But you can call me Cracker Jack."

Surprised laughter broke the tension. His smooth chuckle provided the bass note. Six women began to talk at once, introducing themselves and each other in tones ranging from first soprano to second alto. They found it hilarious that his nickname matched theirs. Divinity, otherwise known as Margaret Mary and her buddy Fudge, originally named Mabel May, had bestowed candy names on everyone. They vied with each other to tell Cracker Jack the whole story of how Bella became Jelly Bean, how Alma became Peanut, how Betty became Butterscotch and how Tillie became Peppermint.

After the hoopla quieted a bit, he asked "And wha'cha doin' here today, ladies?"

"Sittin' and knittin'," Mabel May wisecracked back. Sunlight winked off twelve needles as the women suddenly remembered to take up their work again.

"How come you're knittin'?" he asked.

"We are knitting for a baby," Mabel May replied in her clipped way. This was about to bring on another question until Cracker

Jack paused and took a good look around the circle. As a soldier in the trenches of France he had learned to be very observant.

"Who's expecting?"

Giggles erupted from the women.

"Nobody here" said Peppermint Tillie in her melodious way, "but Buster and Florrie might be. We don't know for sure."

Alma blurted, "And whenever their baby comes, we got to be ready because they asked all of us to be godmothers." Peanut Alma was the smallest, shyest member of the group. She rarely spoke and had never interrupted anyone. Her effort to explain to Jack and the sudden stares of the women brought pink spots to Alma's peanut-textured tan cheeks.

"Who's Buster? Who's Florrie?" asked the scarred man in his mellifluous voice. The ladies sat a little straighter and knitted a little slower as they took turns describing the newlyweds. Jack was a patient listener. Divinity told the long, sweet story of Buster and the shoe. Fudge spun out the romantic tale of Parcheesi games leading to young love. Each godmother chimed in, describing her connection with the happy pair.

"Where'd you godmothers get these pretty yarn colors for the baby?"

This brought forth another story. Fudge described the Sunday afternoon when the Ladies Aid from Portland came to sing and shout about Jesus.

"They said they wanted to come back again, to help us poor old ladies. But I said to them, do you want to know what we really need? Yarn and knittin' needles, that's what. We got us a baby to knit for now, and bunch of sick old folks in need of shawls and lap robes."

"Yep," piped up Peppermint Tillie, "when those African Methodist Episcopal ladies first came here with their socks and soaps, we asked 'em to bring yarn instead. And they did."

Jack gazed slowly around the circle. They could tell he had something on his mind. "It's awful pretty to see you here today, 'specially after all the roughnecks I been with lately. Now I'm wondering if any of you good ladies might be handy with a sewing needle. I don't got me no more clothes than these here," he said, glancing down at his ragged trousers.

Everyone looked toward Tillie in her wheelchair. They knew her as a woman wise in the ways of a needle. Her heavy cheeks jiggled as she grinned and nodded yes.

"I am pleased to say that Miss Peppermint Tillie will help you out with that, Mr. Cracker Jack," announced Fudge. *That woman sounds like a holiness evangelist when she is in a fervor,* thought Margaret Mary. *I do believe there is nothing my friend Mabel May likes more than helping someone.*

The small congregation cheered and shouted Amen.

+++

Alma couldn't resist oddments, the older the better. She collected items that had once been used and loved, then abandoned. Three days later when Cracker Jack appeared again, she was passing three tarnished - once shiny silver - triangular buttons around the circle.

"Lovely to see you dear ladies knitting here in the shade of the cedar grove," he said. "I came by today to extend my deepest thanks to Miss Peppermint Tillie here, and to each one of you fine ladies for helping me become properly outfitted." They *ooohed* and *aaahed* as Jack turned in a slow circle, modeling his new shirt and repaired pants.

"Did you hear we got a note from Florrie and Buster saying they want to come visiting this Sunday?" asked Mabel May.

"I wisht' I coulda been at their wedding," said Jack, sounding wistful.

"Did you hear about the swarm of bees that led the wedding procession?" asked Margaret Mary. "Buster and I said it was a hurricane of happy honeybees."

"And did we tell you about the wedding gifts?" asked Bella. Before Jack could answer, Edna interrupted saying "The lace hankie was my idea."

"I wanted my hair ribbon to be the something blue," blurted Tillie.

"But we all thought Divinity's cologne bottle was a deeper shade of blue," said Fudge.

"Ladies," said Jack. His voice trailed off as the women continued to argue.

"And my hankie was the oldest," protested Bella.

"You can't give a hankie that old," interrupted Alma.

"You can't give something stained," insisted Edna.

"Ladies, ladies." Jack's voice went up in volume and down in register. But the godmothers had their dander up. They didn't take heed.

"My husband's Masonic ring was perfect for borrowed," shouted Mabel May.

"Brides are supposed to borrow, not grooms," protested Tillie.

Jack hitched his crutch under one arm and flapped his hands in an effort to stop the women from talking over each other, but they weren't used to having a referee.

"Ladies. Ladies. LADIES." He sounded like a military commander. The godmothers quieted down, still shooting dirty looks at each other.

"I can only hear one of you at a time," he said, spreading all ten fingers wide and patting the air with his broad palms. "Now, you were telling me," he said, pointing to Tillie. She picked up the story, telling how some people around here thought a romance between a white man and a Negro girl just wasn't proper. Jack laughed in his musical way, showing he wasn't offended.

Glancing at his profile, Margaret Mary saw a soft expression cross his face so she went on to finish the tale. "There's no place for married folks to live here, you know. But Florrie's sister works in Gresham and she found them a furnished room above the bakery."

"I hope Florrie's baking those famous cinnamon cakes of hers," said Edna.

"And I hope Buster found work in the cobbler shop," added Alma.

"I just hope folks in Gresham are nice to that sweet young couple, their skins being such different colors and all..." When self-doubt got ahold of Margaret Mary her voice had a habit of trailing off.

"Wish I'da been at the farm then," said Cracker Jack. Margaret Mary thought he sounded wistful. She heard envy in his tone, too, or maybe it was longing. Whatever it was, the feeling in his voice washed over the knitters, rinsing them with the pleasure of being together. *We are part of something dear,* thought Margaret Mary. *We belong to each other here. Or at least we're beginning to. And he doesn't. Not yet.*

# TWENTY-SEVEN

☙❧

Bad memories have a way of lingering. When a woman's son disappears without a trace, it leaves a wound that never heals. Genealogical research shows no trace of Albert George Wright except his birthdate - February 8, 1892 - the only bit of data on public record. No date or place of marriage was recorded. No date or place of death. Nothing. Margaret Mary's second son simply disappeared. But a mother doesn't stop loving her son no matter what. No matter how mean he acted.

+++

"Tell me about your family," said Ben. He had noticed she didn't volunteer much and wondered if it was a touchy topic. They were sitting side by side on the west porch of the Manor House. The clouds had parted. As the sun sank low, a pale peachy light decorated the side of Margaret Mary's face.

"I'd rather talk about knitting."

"Okay. Tell me about your knitting."

"I'm working on a cable-knit sweater. It's a complicated pattern, hard to explain." Ben's silence encouraged her to go on. "There's a challenge to knitting. There's comfort in it, too. The yarn forms the stitches but the knitting forms the friendships."

"That was a pretty good explanation."

"We tell some pretty good yarns in the Sittin' and Knittin' Group." She grinned at her own joke and he grinned back.

"Have you told them the one about the three Magi visiting you in the infirmary?"

"Heavens no! I don't want those women to think I'm daft. Why do you ask?"

"It's been awhile since you told me about those exotic characters who came to visit and I have some questions."

"Like what?"

"Like what did they bring you? Were they bearing gifts of gold, frankincense or myrhh?"

"Those were for the baby Jesus. Why do you think the Magi would bring anything for a weak old woman?"

"Because that's what Magi do. They bear gifts. What did they give you?" He emphasized You.

She put her chin in her hand and looked pensive. "The will to live?" she asked tentatively.

"Sounds like a pretty good gift. What else?"

"Oh! Yarn and needles from Lily."

The pair sat in satisfied silence in the fading light. After a while Ben asked "Do you ever tell yarns about your family?"

"Which one in my family?" She was stalling for time.

"The one closest to your heart right now."

"That would be my younger boy. The one I haven't seen since... haven't seen for a long time." Her voice caught like a stuck zipper. He waited until she found her breath again.

"My goodness, what day is this?" She raised her eyes to Ben with a startled look.

"February 8th."

"I can't believe it." She shook her head, staring at Ben. "What made you ask about my son right this minute?"

"I have no idea. Why do you ask?"

"Because it's Albert's birthday. And I'd forgotten that. Oh my goodness." She rubbed her eyes, which remained dry.

"So you gave birth how many years ago?"

"I've never been good at math. It was 1892."

"And this is 1937." Ben counted on his fingers. "That was forty-five years ago."

"Forty five years and I remember it like yesterday. I was sore for weeks after that boy was born," she said, glancing at Ben. She'd never talked about childbirth with a man. He nodded in his encouraging way.

"Albert kicked his way into the world and never stopped."

"What was he like as a child?"

"Short on temper and heavy on muscle. Leo was a scrawny boy, no match for his younger brother. The bigger Albert got the harder he was to control. He almost broke Leo's arm once, after his brother turned him in to the sheriff.

"What happened with the sheriff?"

"He said we had to control Albert's mean streak or he'd put him in a school for bad boys. Told us he'd be watching the Wright family real close. George hated that. Said he'd rather leave Billings than be in the sheriff's cross-hairs."

"Did you leave town?"

"We moved to Portland. 1904, it was, just after my youngest boy started telling everyone to call him Bull. Told us Albert was a sissy name."

"Bull?"

"George liked pit bull dogs, said our boy was like a pit bull. Any kind of upset would bring out the bite in him. Albert's dad admired our boy's feistiness."

"Like a pit bull," Ben repeated in a low voice.

"Dogs always got upset around Albert. Whenever the dogs in the neighborhood came to a sudden boil, I knew my son was bothering them."

"Did he like school?" Ben headed for a safer topic.

"No, he was a poor student, expelled from high school so many times we finally gave up. At sixteen we let him quit school. He hired on at the brickyard but the boss fired him before long."

"What did he do after that?"

"Stayed out half the night. I'd bundle up and go out in the dark to watch for him, pacing and worrying. Where is that boy? Breaking into garages, or something worse? Neighbors complained of missing tools and bikes but he denied taking things. I told him he must not steal. That's one of the Ten Commandments, I told him."

"You did your best," Ben said softly. She went on as if he hadn't spoken. "One summer night I woke up to hear George shouting that Albert was acting like a thief. I wrapped my bathrobe around my middle and went into the living room to see what was going on and heard George yell "Where have you been all night?"

"Nowhere."

"The police came looking for you."

"When?"

"After midnight."

"Did they find Ernie?"

"What were you and Ernie up to?"

"Did they find my bag?"

"What is going on here, Albert? Tell me..."

"Don't tell the police anything."

'You're nothing but a thief!' George was shouting and my heart was kicking like a rat in a lunchbox. Albert pushed his dad away. When I tried to stop him he shoved me against the doorjamb and ran into the night."

Margaret Mary rubbed her clavicle with both hands. "That was the last time I saw my son," she added in a small voice. "July 10, 1910. He was eighteen. I can still see the way he slouched, wouldn't meet my eyes." She dropped her face into her hands and shivered with the memory.

"I can feel the tug of it," said Ben, "your love for your boy. And your disappointment in the way he was acting."

"Yes," she said slowly. "I do love Albert despite his violent ways. I haven't laid eyes on him for... How long, Ben?"

He did the math. "Twenty seven years."

"My goodness, he's been gone twenty seven years. It's odd how I half remember Albert in my heart and half forget him in my mind."

The sun had set behind a bank of charcoal clouds. They sat quietly, watching a band of pale apricot light lingering at the horizon. When she spoke, the words were almost too soft for Ben to hear. "I know my son is not a sparrow but I hope God is keeping an eye on him anyway."

"How do you pray for your missing son?"

"I pray don't be in jail. That's what I've been saying to the Holy Mother all these years. Don't let him be in prison. That's how I pray. Please don't let him be dead."

"I'll join you in those prayers," murmured Ben. His voice was thick as cream.

They breathed together in the darkening air. Eventually she went on. "I don't know where Albert is now, but my love for him is here," she said, placing a hand over her heart. "And the lumps of his fighting ways are here," she added, touching her breastbone.

Ben rose and stood behind her chair. He rested warm hands on her shoulders and his tender touch gave her the confidence to say it.

"My truest prayer" she whispered, "is to see Albert sitting in the summer sun with his little boy, fishing off the end of a dock. I pray for my son to show his son how to hold the pole, cast the line and reel in the trout."

# TWENTY-EIGHT

ଓଞ୦

Cordelia, her daughter-in-law, trudged up the lane from Halsey Street. She held the hands of Dean and Virginia, her youngest grandchildren.

"Hello, hello," they called.

Margaret Mary waved with both arms. They'd sent a letter saying the family would come by trolley on Sunday afternoon. She was perched expectantly on the porch chair.

"My goodness, it's good to see you."

All four Wrights agreed that it was.

"And isn't the sky clear today."

They agreed on this, too.

Dean, acting shy, stood apart as his sister tried to sit on the old woman's lap. "You're too big for that now," warned Cordelia. Virginia tried wiggling into the wicker chair as they used to do, but Grandmother's wide hips filled it. Pushing playfully, the children jumped about on top of the porch wall. Margaret Mary watched nervously. To her they looked precarious but their mother didn't seem worried.

"What grade are you in now, Dean?"

"Third." He gnawed on a thumbnail.

"What do you like best about it?"

"Recess." With that her eight-year-old grandson hopped off the wall and ran down the steps.

"How is school, Virginia?"

"I'm in the fifth grade now at Rigler."

"What are you studying?"

"Long division. It's hard."

"What else?"

"Geography. I like that."

"Who is your teacher this year?"

"Miss Bennett. She's usually nice, but strict sometimes."

Cordelia reported what was going on in the Wright household. Leo was hunting for work. Jim's wages were supporting the family. His leg had healed, the one he broke stopping a runaway toboggan on Mt. Hood. He met Mildred on the church youth trip and she'd come to see him while his leg was in a cast. Everyone could see they were in love. Jim had asked Mildred to marry him and she'd said yes. Margo was in Salem, working her way through college and rarely came home. Virginia was a Girl Scout. Dean played softball. Cordelia was scraping to make ends meet. The Ladies Guild of Acreage Church helped out by bringing macaroni, parsnips and spuds.

Family chat soon ran out of steam. Virginia ran down the steps and scratched a hopscotch pattern in the dirt, singing softly as she jumped, balanced on one foot and jumped again. Dean threw rocks at trees, birds and squirrels. An easy silence stretched between the women, content to watch the youngsters play and think their own thoughts. The east wind blew steadily, keeping at them until Cordelia pulled up her collar, called the children and headed for the trolley. By the time they'd reached Halsey Street and turned to wave, Margaret Mary had taken refuge indoors.

+++

A nap was in order but her mind was in disorder. She saw herself as she'd once been, as Maggie Aggie playing hopscotch. She recalled the magic of the numbered squares and how fine it felt to get to heaven, but could not come up with any clear memory of how to play the game. *Why in the world can I not remember how this game progresses? Once upon a time I knew the rules of hopscotch and how the penalties work. Now it's all gone. I have no idea how to play the game my granddaughter knows by heart.*

It worries her, this small erosion of memory. *Where did they go, the intricacies of the girlhood game I once knew so well? What does this mean?* Fear of losing her memory reminded her of a time at the beach when she'd walked into the surf expecting a solid surface but plunged into a deep hole in the sand. Today she was sputtering in the same sort of confusion. *It feels like the ground is shifting under me. This will never do.*

Margaret Mary concentrated fiercely on hopscotch. She directed her mind's eye back to the wagon-rutted streets where she'd grown up. Hay in rural Ontario, Canada. She hadn't thought of her birthplace in ages. *Hay is such a funny name for a town.* Her muscles twitched as her memory jumped in the summer sun. Names and faces eluded her but she could still hear children's voices. Come on, Maggie Aggie, they would call, come and play hopscotch. *All right, I admit it. I can't remember the rules. But did hopscotch teach me anything?*

*Hopscotch taught me to play fair. That's it. With the lines we drew in the dirt we spelled out some good ways to live. We improvised and we played fair. We worked out rules that gave everyone an equal chance to win.*

So, all is not lost. Something of value remains. These were comforting thoughts. *But it's so odd that I've forgotten so much.* She couldn't let it go.

*What must a player do to win?*
*How does she get to heaven?*
*When someone loses the game does she have to go to hell?*
*Does hopscotch have a purgatory?*

# TWENTY-NINE

☙❧

The twisted old man named Joshua sat with his head in his hands. Margaret Mary took a chair at the end of the porch, not wanting to disturb his reverie. On this warm September day she was content to sit quietly and observe the passing scene. Presently a bearded man in a black hat approached. He looked like a rabbi.

Joshua stood up, or tried to, but his back was askew. "That's fine, my dear man. No need to rise. Here, I will sit beside you." Rabbi Abrahamson introduced himself and pulled up a chair at a little distance from Margaret Mary. He nodded in her direction, wiped his ruddy face with a pale linen handkerchief and smiled at Joshua. The twisted man looked none to happy to see him.

"The High Holy Days are not usually so hot for us here in Oregon," the rabbi said. He spoke with a Yiddish accent that was both familiar and repellant to Joshua, who turned away from the rabbi's beaming countenance. The bent man hardened his eyes and looked toward the distant tree line then growled "What do you want with me?"

"No need to be rude, my good man." Rabbi Abrahmanson gazed into Joshua's face with a warm openness. "I recognized you as a fellow Jew and simply stopped to rest a moment. I am on my way to the director's office to learn which room we may use to hold our High Holy Day services."

Although Joshua Herschel had grown up in an observant home and knew about Jewish rituals it had been many years since he had observed Holy Days. They were solemn occasions for soul-searching but he didn't want any part of that now. He had made too many mistakes.

"Here?" Joshua blurted. "You're bringing Rosh Hashanah services to this place?"

"Yes, indeed," said the rabbi, "and Yom Kippur as well." His big grin parted his dark beard. "You are not forgotten here, my friend. The idea of Jews at the Poor Farm is very surprising to many people in Portland. But you are not alone here. I would be a rich man if I had a dime for everyone who blurts 'You mean to say there are Jewish paupers at the Multnomah County Poor Farm!'

"Are you telling me there are other Jews in this place?" The incredulous look on Joshua's face widened the rabbi's smile.

"Yes, come to services on Rosh Hashanah and you will meet them. It's hard to find our people among the six hundred souls living in this place." He spoke with assurance and warmth. The rabbi's dark eyes appraised Joshua. The old man squirmed under holy scrutiny.

"You made a mistake." Rabbi Abrahamson stated it simply, as if reporting a fact.

It was true. This man had his number.

"In the Talmud," the rabbi reminded him, "it says you're not expected to be perfect. But you're not permitted to stop trying, either." Joshua nodded uneasily. "As you know, Jews don't subscribe to the notion of original sin. We believe that people are born pure and have a chance to be pure again each day." Joshua nodded again. He was paying attention despite himself. "I don't speak of sin," the rabbi went. "I prefer the word transgression. God will forgive you for your transgressions but you have a lot of atonement to do first, my good man."

"When you're in the poorhouse," muttered Joshua, "every day is a day of atonement." Their eyes met. Both men nodded in mutual understanding.

"You know what to do," the rabbi went on, speaking so tenderly that Joshua turned away to hide the sudden wetness in his eyes.

After pausing to let the bent man collect himself, the rabbi spoke. "You know what you've done, and you know what to do next. The High Holy Days give you a chance to start over. Now is the time to acknowledge the wrongs you've done to your friends, your family and your faith."

"I have made a lot of mistakes," Joshua admitted, heaving a sigh and shifting in his chair.

"Mistakes go with being human, my dear man. So if you want another chance, if you want to wake up clear, then you have to do the work. But you don't have to do it alone. Will I see you on Rosh Hashanah and Yom Kippur?"

Joshua seemed too emotional to speak. Margaret Mary saw him nod yes. She sensed the weight of guilt lifting off his twisted shoulders.

+++

"I couldn't help overhearing," she said after the rabbi left.

"I was afraid of that."

"As the man said, we've all made mistakes. I sure have."

"Like what?"

"Like losing a son, and then losing a husband."

"Losing?"

"They left. They didn't want to live with me."

"Men leave women for all sorts of reasons. Maybe it wasn't your fault."

When she didn't answer Joshua went on. "I left, too, left my people. I was so stubborn back then, wanted things my way. Uncle Sol and I didn't get along."

"So where'd your mistake come in?"

"So dumb." Joshua shook his head as if trying to get ants out of his hair. "I made a wrong turn, got in with a bunch of gambling men. Bingo, slot machines, the numbers. Lost the business..."

"Lost what business?"

"Dry cleaning shop. Herschel's at 12th and Washington. Been in the family since 1904." He shook his head again, a nervous habit.

"When things are going good, it's like you're a self-made man. When things go sour, when you're boarding up the shop, you feel like a self-ruined man. It's gone now, all gone..."

"I'm sorry," she said softly.

Joshua's bristly chin brushed his chest.

"You're not alone," Margaret Mary said after a while.

"Yeah, that's what the rabbi said."

"Will you take him up on the invitation and go to those services?"

"Don't know...."

+++

Three days later Margaret Mary was drawn outdoors by the sound of harmonica music. She wasn't the only one. Two scruffy guys leaned low against the shady side of the porch, smoking. One had a nicked face, as if he shaved with a hatchet. She recognized Lex and Cox, the ones Ben and Bella said might be Reds. *What are they up to with their heads together like that, talking in low voices? Planning to organize the farm workers to go on strike?* She hated the idea of that. Things were going well around the Farm these days and she wanted it to stay peaceful. Whether Lex and Cox were Commies or not, she felt edgy around them. *Why are these ruffians sneaking sideways glances at the crippled man?*

Joshua sat hunched, hands to his mouth, playing with full focus. She didn't recognize the tune, something mournful. He did not look up as she approached. *Probably can't move his twisted neck,* she figured, settling into a wide wicker chair. *Or maybe he's too caught up in that sorrowful song to notice anything else.*

"That sounded like a lament," she said after the last notes faded off.

"An old Jewish tune my grandfather taught me," Joshua replied. "Came out of the ghetto at Minsk way back in the olden days."

"It's haunting, makes me want to cry."

"My people had to learn how to turn weeping into dancing," he said with a crooked smile. "Only way to survive."

She nodded, too moved to trust her voice.

"This harmonica is a beauty," he said, lifting it like a trophy. "Much finer than my first one, the mouth organ I built for myself."

Margaret Mary smiled, encouraging Joshua to go on.

"Yes," he grinned, "when I was a kid I made my own mouth harp." His smile was both shy and proud. "For hours I'd squat on the curb listening to the men play their mouth organs. They played every song by ear. I knew I had to make music like that."

"How does a boy make his own mouth organ?" she asked. "I can't picture it."

"Made it out of junk," he said, face shining. "I got me an empty tin can, bent it in the middle, cut a bit of rubber and tied it round with twine. I waited until Uncle Sol was snoring then snuck his knife out of his pants pocket and cut a hole in the rubber. After running it across my mouth hundreds of times, I learned to make a bit of music. The sound coming out of the little hole would change as I moved my mouth. I like to think I coaxed a few songs out of it."

"I never heard of such a thing," she exclaimed.

"My mother hated the noise I made with it but she must of heard something that made her stick up for me. 'This boy needs a real mouth harp,' she said to Uncle Sol."

Joshua's voice softened to a hush. "That was the first time she ever stuck up for me."

"I'm so glad to hear your mother recognized your talent."

Her heart flickered, thinking about her own son. *Could Albert have been musical and I never noticed it?* Half afraid to follow this train of thought, afraid it would derail her composure, Margaret Mary focused on Joshua again.

"Then what happened?" she asked, a little more urgently than necessary.

"She kept after him until Uncle Sol bought me my first real mouth harp. It cost ten cents, a lot of money in those days. When I started working as a tailor's apprentice and got to earning a little money I bought me a better harmonica and passed that first mouth harp on to my nephew David. Musical talent runs in the family. Then when the dry cleaning business got going good, I bought myself a twelve-hole instrument with three octaves on it. I learned everything by ear. Here's one of my favorites."

Joshua swung into a jazzy version of *Button Up Your Overcoat*.

"This chromatic Hohner is my pride and joy," he said, holding it up for Margaret Mary to admire. "Don't know how I'd get through hard times without my harmonica."

With that the old man raised it to his mouth and began to blow *I Want To Be Loved By You*. Her good foot couldn't help tapping along.

# THIRTY

༄༅

By mid-November everyone in the Manor House was depressed. The inmates hadn't seen the sun for weeks. Black clouds climbed on the shoulders of the last storm, rain poured from the heavens and earth tried to absorb more water. When Margaret Mary stepped out onto the porch for a breath of fresh air, Tillie and Jack were talking about the hardships of their days. Ben joined the group and widened the topic of conversation. "This gloomy weather has me thinking about regrets. What would you say you regret most in your life before you got here?"

Margaret Mary had been thinking about that very thing, the boy she'd loved and lost so long ago. *How does Ben always know what's weighing heavy on my heart, how I worry over my youngest son. So many regrets since the boy ran away from home. But I can't tell anyone about my part in that.* She gulped and turned away so nobody would see the sheen of sweat on her skin.

"I'd have to say the war." Jack, the most outgoing of the four, jumped right in. "I went to France with big ideas, went through the business of artillery training until a cannon backfired, took out my eye and blasted away my toes. Then I went through all the business of hospitals and learning to walk with a crutch. I still wanted to go back to the unit. 'You're not a very good soldier, are you,' my sergeant said. He told me I better stick to singing."

"How'd you start to sing?" asked Ben.

"I sang my way through my Army time," Jack went on. "Frenchmen understood that, but not Americans. My service buddies were just poor, ornery people like me. I could sing before I could talk, learned songs on my mama's lap, then from the radio, then at Band of Hope revival meetings."

"Revivals," said Tillie, trying to interrupt, but Jack barreled on. He was on a roll.

"My people in Kentucky, they were a boisterous, whiskey-drinking bunch, the rowdiest singing and fighting people in the Appalachians. They liked to cook up alcoholic beverages without government approval. Bootleggers, you'd call 'em. When I was a kid I hung around the stills, singing for nickels. But the years fell hard on me, smashed me down. Now I'm flat broke. No one pays attention to an old soldier that got hurt. Here I am sixty-two years old and I never dealt with respectable people until I got here to meet you good folks…"

The other three took that in without comment. Margaret Mary enjoyed Jack's compliment. She liked being seen as one of the good folks.

The large, lopsided woman in the wheelchair jumped in to the conversation. "Thinking of revival meetings brings up my biggest regret. It's about music, too," said Tillie. "I wish I coulda sung for my living. I loved watching the player piano when I was a girl, keys rising and falling by themselves as we sang about Jesus. Then I got to be an usher, laboring along on my bad ankles, passing out folded-paper fans from Montgomery's Mortuary. But what I really wanted to do was push the preacher out of the way, stand up tall and sing my heart out."

A nervous cough took her voice. Sweat shined on her doughy face. Tillie began twisting her heavy hair and pulling with both hands. *I still think her hair looks like peppermint candy,* thought Margaret Mary, as the agitated woman yanked on mud-colored hair streaked with white.

"When did you first begin to sing?" Ben asked.

"When did I first begin to breathe!" she retorted. "When did I first begin to walk and talk! I was a singer from my first days on earth," asserted Tillie. "I kept on singing when I went to work scrubbing floors. You got to work with your hands," she said, spreading them wide for emphasis. "I worked as a factory hand, stitching shirts, worked as a domestic, washed finery and cooking pots in the houses of rich folks until my legs gave out. But come Sunday I sang free. Morning, noon and night I went to services at any church you could name on the north side of Portland. I loved to sing the wonders of God. But if I'm not in church, I gotta use my hands when I wanta sing!"

Everyone nodded. They could see her callused hands. They could understand what Tillie was talking about.

"You can't stop singing," Jack affirmed. "Neither can I. It's in our blood."

Ben cleared his throat. "Your talk of singing reminds me of my wife. Reminds me of my biggest regret. It makes me wish I could do my life differently." His voice was tentative. "If I had it to do all over again I wouldn't kill my wife."

Shock shot through the group like a bullet. Mouths dropped open. All three turned to stare at their mild-mannered friend.

"What happened? Did you hit her?" asked Jack.

"I never laid my hands on her. Never."

Ben swallowed, emphasizing the point with his fist. "But there are other ways to kill a woman." His breath grew ragged. "Many ways. And not all require the use of force. The way I killed Laura was worse. Slower."

Nobody spoke. Nobody moved. No one dared take a breath.

"In truth," Ben said, "I don't want to talk about it."

His face was grim.
His gait was urgent.
He vanished into the night.
They sat in stunned silence under the dark sky.
There was no moon.

# THIRTY-ONE

ଓଃଃ

There was all sorts of unhappiness around the Poor Farm that winter. Margaret Mary could not imagine Ben harming anyone. It was simply not possible for her friend to hurt a flea, let alone a woman. A wife.

If she had been able to peer into the minds of various people that week, peeked into their secret depths, she would have found an assortment of human miseries.

Hazel Parker, for one. Hazel had found a lump in her left breast and was in a state of panic about the dark terror facing her. Was she going to die? She was afraid of doctors. Who could she tell? She turned to whisper to Bella in the next bed, only to find her friend asleep, leaving Hazel alone with her fear of certain death.

Across the tracks from the Manor House in a sprawling old tavern on the outskirts of Troutdale, Cracker Jack Smith sat in a dark booth. He smoked cigarettes and listened to the boozy talk of a dozen men hunched on stools along the bar. What a comfort the Lucky Strikes could be. When he gave up smoking seven years earlier, he had not been able to conceive of a situation that might cause him to start up again. But then this business with Ben had come along.

And the Superintendent of the Manor House, BB Jackson, was feeling acutely miserable. Not because some of the inmates called him Big Boss or because they laughed behind his back when he got riled up and sprayed little pellets of spit as he talked. "Should call him MG for Machine Gun instead of BB for single shot," said one old soldier. No, Mr. Jackson knew nothing of this, nor of Ben's regrets or Hazel's fears. His misery was of an illicit, romantic nature.

His wife Doris, of whom he was half afraid, had been postponing a visit to her mother for the past three weeks. This required BB to keep postponing his first extra-marital liaison. Miss Lizzie DeLuca was a teacher - quite a few years younger - and he was seriously infatuated with her. They met when she brought three journalism students from Pacific University to write a feature article on the Poor Farm. The article had been very flattering to the Superintendent. He couldn't stop thinking about the curvaceous Lizzie and to his great surprise she said she found him attractive, too.

Today Mrs. Doris Jackson had finally boarded the train to Hermiston to spend the week with her elderly mother and Mr. BB Jackson had finally gone to dinner at the home of the luscious Lizzie. Things had not gone well. The awkward evening ended in her half-darkened living room. He was not the lothario she thought he was, not the man he'd hoped to be. As he rose from the couch, touching her shoulder apologetically, she smiled gamely through her disappointment.

BB couldn't shake the image of Lizzie, shapely in a red dress, rapidly blinking her small black-olive eyes, her face in shadow as she stood at the door. The porch light had formed a halo around her frizzy dark hair.

And there was more.

Half a mile away from Edgefield, unnoticed, the Columbia River moved rapidly, dark currents swirling in silence around unseen rocks. The moon, indistinct behind thin clouds, formed a round platter of some ill-defined brightness in the hazy sky. Part of this light came through the window near Margaret Mary's bed where, three cots away, poor Hazel lay afraid and awake.

A bit of moonlight leaked onto another cot where Joshua Herschel was suffering another toothache. His back molar, which had given him trouble before, throbbed in the dark. He placed the cool metal harmonica against his lower jaw. This helped for a little while, until his feverish skin warmed up the Hohner.

A beam of moonlight gleamed on the roof of the tavern where Cracker Jack Smith was pondering his regrets. He leaned his chin into one hand and told a grizzled guy at the bar about the time he'd convinced his little sister to let him baptize her. "I tol' Sissie I'd take her down to the branch and sprinkle her in the name of God," he said. "An' I did as promised. I had her kneel down in the dirt and said the right words, I baptize you in the name of the Father, the Son and the Holy Ghost." Jack waved his arms like a Pentecostal preacher and caught his reflection in the dirty mirror behind the bar. "Then," he paused, trying not to slur his words, "I peed on her head. Three times. I tol' Sissie a warm sprinkling was better than cold."

Jack's listener hardly responded. Maybe he was too far gone on whisky, or maybe he'd heard worse stories.

"Wanna know what happened next?" asked Jack, poking the man's shoulder. "Yup," came the dull reply.

"Sissie told on me, of course. And Pappy took me to the woodshed with his razor strop. She got baptized by warm pee, but I got baptized by fire."

+++

But Margaret Mary didn't know about the miseries other folks were suffering. She didn't know about Jack's regrets or

Superintendent Jackson's impotence or Joshua's toothache. She couldn't get the fright of Ben's words out of her mind. Then to make it worse, something terrible happened. She hated confrontations and had always tried her best to avoid them but she ran into trouble that afternoon in the knitting group.

"Margaret Mary, what do you think?" Tillie demanded as soon as she walked in. She was alarmed to realize a kind of poll was evidently taking place. Teams were getting drawn within the group.

"Oh heavens," she'd stammered, attempting to bide her time. "Well, my goodness. Anything's possible, I suppose."

"But do you believe him?" Mabel May's voice cut like a paring knife. "That's what I want to know. Do you believe Ben?"

All eyes were upon her. She hated having the Sittin' and Knittin' group see how uncertain she was.

"Well, I've never known Ben to lie," she murmured.

"People lie all the time," said Mabel May. "Honestly, where have you been?"

Her face grew hot; she felt her skin turn crimson.

In Margaret Mary's account of life no one schemed or lied. No one was greedy or mean-spirited. In her book everyone was a decent sort. She pursed her lips and swallowed hard.

"I don't believe people lie all the time. But if you are forcing me to take a stand..." Her voice trembled. Attempting to cover this, she spoke rather loudly. "Then I will stand behind Ben." It was the strongest statement she had been known to make in her many conversations with the knitting women. The toll it took on her was evident in her still-burning face. "Now, if you will excuse me," she said, "I have something to do."

Her legs went wobbly. She was afraid she would stumble on her way out of the sitting room. At the last minute, as she moved successfully through the blur of women and chairs, she caught Bella's eye. She saw a beacon of kindness in the midst of chaos, such an expression of understanding on this round Italian face that the thought flicked through her mind. *I have a friend, a true friend.*

She kept going over it in her mind, musing. *Most of them did the best they could. Isn't that fair to say? Most of the Poor Farm people did the best they could.* She wanted to think the best of people, even when they didn't act their best.

PART THREE

# MARGARET MARY

೦ಶ೮೦

# COMING HOME

*1938*

# THIRTY-TWO

☙☜

"Ben, listen to me...." It was a week later. Winter solstice had come and gone. The rains hadn't stopped. She'd been watching for her friend. Here he came, head down, unshaved. His puffy violet-veined eyelids and pale face pained her. She got right to the point.

"Ben, you've been on my mind night and day. You know I won't find fault with you. We've all made mistakes, we've all got regrets. You were the one who brought up this idea of talking about regrets, so you must have wanted to get it off your chest. In my church we call that going to confession. I'm no priest, definitely not."

She took a big breath and swallowed hard. Ben kept his chin close to his chest, not meeting her eye.

"I'm here to listen, not to judge. I am your friend, Ben. We all are." She stopped to draw another breath. "This may be the longest speech I've made in my life."

"I'll think about it." Ben's voice was raspy. The wind lifted his thinning hair as he moved away, the skin of his scalp deepening from pink to crimson.

Her heart lifted in sympathy for her friend. *I hope he believes me.*

Behold the Lamb of God who taketh away the sins of the world, she said under her breath, repeating words of the mass from the Roman Missal. Mother Mary, she murmured as she fingered the beads of her Rosary, help Ben know he can trust me with his secrets.

Again that night she sat on the porch with Tillie and Jack. By unspoken agreement, the friends had gathered in the same spot every evening since Ben's shocking revelation. They kept hoping he would show up. Tonight he did.

As Ben climbed the steps his jaw was set with determination. He glanced up to see expressions of kindness on three faces. Tillie reached out and brushed his arm. Ben kept clearing his throat. He had never heard such a respectful silence.

They looked into his eyes, as if Ben had just told them, at this very moment, that he loved each and every one of them.

Margaret Mary heard him take a deep breath. The others straightened their backs. Ben's eyes filled but no tears fell as long as he kept blinking fast enough. As much as he hated having to talk about this, these were his friends. A huge tide of sadness waited to wash over him. The life he'd ruined hadn't been entirely his own.

They waited quietly. Ben flared his nostrils and began.

"I used to drink too much. My wife didn't like me coming home drunk," Ben's words came slowly. "And I smoked." He paused. "Laura used to sing in the kitchen. She had a lovely voice. Cigarette smoke made her cough."

"But I don't understand why you say you killed her," said Tillie. Her pale eyes, nearly hidden in her fleshy face, were filled with questions.

"Because that's what I did. I killed her slowly. Laura got sick, asthma I think...." He spoke in a strangled voice. "She was glad when I finally got work at the mill but it upset her when I got fired for showing up drunk. The money dried up. She stopped singing...."

"Oh," murmured Margaret Mary sympathetically. The others kept quiet, listening with all their might.

"Laura would cry and gasp for breath. I don't remember it very well, but she was always gasping. I hated going home at night." Ben talked on for almost an hour. The three friends didn't move, just sat there absorbing his words.

Ben stopped to mop his face with a red bandana handkerchief. It was unusually warm for a winter night in Oregon. "They ran me a tab at the bar. Laura hated it when I came home drunk. She begged me to stop."

"I can see why you'd regret that," said Margaret Mary. Her voice was thin. Hearing about Ben's wife reminded her how hard it had been living with George, how often she'd felt the same way he said Laura did.

"I begged people to lend me money but there was never enough to pay the bills. The house was always cold and damp. One night my wife got down on her knees and begged me to buy coal. Begged me. I stopped going home."

"But that doesn't mean you killed her," said Cracker Jack.

"Yes, I did," Ben asserted.

"Laura choked to death one night while I was out on a bender. I did kill my wife. I killed her. With neglect."

He looked at each of them in turn. "Don't you see?" he asked, head tilted forward.

"See what?" asked Jack.

"That I'm a sinner."

"Oh, Ben," said Tillie, "we all are."

The wind was still. The sound of Ben's confession poured into the soil. The good earth was absorbing every word.

"Come now," intoned Jack after a while. "Come now, let us set things straight, saith the Lord. Though your sins be like scarlet, they may become white as snow."

Nobody took a breath for the longest time.

"Whose words are those?" asked Ben.

"The prophet Isaiah," replied Jack. "Chapter one, verse eighteen."

"Say it again, will you?"

"Come now, let us set things straight, saith the Lord. Though your sins be like scarlet, they may become white as snow."

"Where'd you learn Isaiah?"

"In an Army hospital, from a chaplain. He said the docs could patch up my body but only God could mend my soul. Gave me this verse to memorize."

Margaret Mary glanced up as Ben slumped in his chair, face crumpling. She spotted tears trembling on his eyelashes, then a spill running down his cheeks. He bent from the waist, covered his face with both hands and sobbed like a child.

After a time, Tillie and Jack shifted position. Margaret Mary realized it was a signal. They were getting ready for something. They clearly knew that something was coming, but it surprised her when they began to hum. She didn't recognize the melody. Tillie led off in her coppery alto. Jack joined in, humming in a way that reminded Margaret Mary of the sound gold makes when it's melting.

Ben's shuddery sobs gave way to sighs, then to stillness.

After a time the duo began to sing, putting words to the tune they'd been humming. What poured out of their mouths was delicate but confident, too, as if it came straight from their hearts. *"You got to cross that lonesome valley,"* they sang, ever so tenderly. *"Cross that lonesome valley, Ben ... you got to cross it, yes you do, but not all by yourself, we're here to walk with you..."*

*How do they do that*, she wondered, *improvising new words to old hymn verses without missing a beat.* Her eyes spilled with tears to hear Peppermint Tillie and Cracker Jack harmonizing as if they'd been singing together forever.

PART THREE : MARGARET MARY COMING HOME | 1938

A flock of swallows burst out from under the eaves, unable to stay in their roost when such heavenly sounds were rising into the night sky. When the harmonies trailed off into silence, a few fallen leaves were the only things that remained in motion.

# THIRTY-THREE

༺༻

"Cats are too sly," said Mabel May, pulling her face into a scowl.

"Where'd you get that idea?" Margaret Mary tried to keep the impatience out of her voice.

"Inherited it. Where I grew up, everyone knew cats were the sneakiest animals on earth."

"Well, if you'd known my Ginger Cat you'd have different ideas. She was the most graceful cat in..."

"I still say cats are too sneaky to be trusted" said Mabel May in that insistent way of hers.

So Margaret Mary hid the living ball of fur under her sweater and sneaked it into the infirmary. She hoped the kitten would be a solace to Rhoda, suffering with cancer of the bones. "It's a calico come to visit," she announced in a cheery tone, placing the kitten on the bed.

"We Brits call that a tortoiseshell," called Lily White as she passed by. "A much more elegant term, wouldn't you say?" Margaret Mary would. She found this kitten irresistible no matter what you called it, calico or tortoiseshell. She adored its bright orange fur with splotches of brown and black. It had a white belly and bib, four tiny white socks and bit of white at the tip of the tail. She thought Rhoda would find the calico-tortoiseshell kitten irresistible, too.

"Ohhhh," purred the patient, "aren't you just the sweetest little thing."

The kitten was homeless like the inmates - and an orphan to boot - but none of those hardships showed in her bearing. She held her head high and walked confidently down the length of Rhoda's body.

"I'll call her Marigold," announced Rhoda, "because they're the kind of flowers that can thrive anywhere."

With that, Marigold nodded and curled up beneath Rhoda's chin as if to show she was ready to bloom and grow right here in the sick ward.

"It's not healthy to have an animal here." Nurse Bessie's voice was steely. "I simply will not have a litter box in a ward already furnished with bed pans."

Margaret Mary had been so excited about cheering up Rhoda she hadn't considered the nurses.

Luckily, Dr. Conrad Furst adored felines. He couldn't resist a creature so young, so lovely and so homeless. Exercising the authority of Medical Director he managed to convince the nursing staff, though none of the inmates knew how he did it. He saw to it that a casement window was always propped open. He showed the kitten how to come and go as needed. So Marigold was allowed to stay, not only as company for the sick woman but for her sanity too. Everybody could see how the bone cancer had brought her spirits low.

"You began to get better the day you got the tortoiseshell," said Lily White the next day. "Why is that, now?"

"Rats!" said Rhoda. The word came out on a spray of spit, though it didn't go far enough to splatter Margaret Mary who was standing at the foot of the bed.

"Rats?" asked Lily, tilting her head toward one shoulder.

## PART THREE : MARGARET MARY COMING HOME | 1938

"When the pains are bad it feels like I have rats gnawing at my bones. And I won't give in to no dirty rats," said Rhoda, squaring her jaw and squinting her eyes.

"How do rats help you get better?" Lily looked mystified. Margaret Mary stood speechless.

"At night when the pains thrash down my legs, I say to myself the rats have come. Time to fight them. And then I fight with all I've got."

"I do admire your willpower, luv," said Lily, saluting the patient on her way out.

+++

A curious thing happened to Margaret Mary as she told Ben about this. She admitted she had begun to feel differently toward Rhoda. "Until now I kept visiting her to show Lily I could stick with it," she said, "But there was no pleasure in it for me."

"None?" asked Ben. He looked as if he didn't believe that for one minute.

"The only pleasure was in using my willpower. Lily admires willpower. As long as I kept showing up and being nice to a woman I didn't like, I felt good about myself. Noble, even."

"What about gossip?" he asked with a sideways grin. "What about the pleasure of collecting stories about Rhoda to entertain your friends?"

"Oh. About the rats, you mean?"

"That's the most recent example," he nodded, "not to mention the bed pan incident."

She dropped her chin and fell silent, nervously fanning her face with both hands. "You caught me," she said after a while. "I started gossiping about Rhoda after she sat on my glasses." She glanced at Ben to read his mood, hoping he wouldn't say I told you so. He didn't. Instead, he asked, "So, why do you say you're feeling differently about Rhoda now?"

"Because of what I saw today."

"What was that?"

"I watched that lovely little calico press her cheek against Rhoda's, rubbing her soft fur into the wrinkles. She's so smart. She can tell Rhoda craves touch and Marigold is such a generous toucher. She even kissed Rhoda on the lips. If an orphan kitten can be that affectionate with such a difficult woman, then maybe I can be a little more generous, too."

# THIRTY-FOUR

ଔଃ

"It seems we've got some Communists on the farm," said Ben. "They're talking like bullies, stirring up trouble."

"How do you know that?" asked Bella.

"The chow line moved liked molasses tonight so I had plenty of time to listen while a couple of rough characters made their pitch about a sit-down strike. Remember those guys we saw in the barnyard, Margaret Mary? That time when they made the other farmhands pitch coins into the circle so they could buy booze?"

Margaret Mary tightened her shoulders at the memory. "Lex and Cox. The same ones who spit on Jasper."

Her throat had gone dry. "What did you hear?" she croaked.

"They were talking about clothes at first, how Lex got his winter coat off an undertaker by shoveling snow at a mortuary. Then he held up his foot, poked at the wet cardboard in the sole of his shoe, and said none of the stiffs had feet the right size to fit him. Cox said we'd all be wearing good boots and eating sirloin instead of turnip stew if this farm was run right."

"I don't like to hear about taking clothes off a dead man," shuddered Bella.

"That didn't seem to bother Cox," said Ben. "He kept complaining that Roosevelt's New Deal is a raw deal for guys like us, how this isn't exactly the land of the free. How the Commies are better at running the country than the President. How inmates at Edgefield would be a lot better off if the Reds took over here."

"What do you think they meant, Ben?"

"Unemployment councils," he replied. "They told how the Communist Party has set up councils to assist unemployed men all over the country. I've heard about this, too, how the Reds are trying to stop people from being evicted when they can't pay the rent. They told of one city where Party members stand by while constables are hauling furniture to the curb. Once the constables are gone the Communists carry everything back in, set up the kids' beds right where they were and escort the family back into the house."

"That sounds very kind," said Bella.

Margaret Mary was worrying about a sit-down strike. "I've heard about strikes on the radio," she said, "but I didn't know the Communists were behind them."

"I'm not sure they are, not all of the strikes, anyway," added Ben. "Meat packers at Hormel, maybe, and probably at the Goodyear factory, but not the baseball players in Ohio. Here's the kicker, though. Lex and Cox said that if this farm were being run right, we'd all be wearing good boots, smoking fine tobacco and drinking aged whiskey. They're trying to talk the farmhands into holding a sit-down strike."

"And were the men listening?" asked Margaret Mary.

"Yes," he nodded. "A lot of guys in the chow line were paying very close attention."

The threat of a work strike left Margaret Mary more agitated than she'd been in a long time. She got all tongue-tied and had to excuse herself, leaving Bella and Ben to hash things out. It upset her, the prospect of troublemakers convincing farm workers - men she knew - to sit down and refuse to work. She felt strongly opposed to the idea but couldn't say why. It made her throat so dry that even three glasses of water didn't do a thing.

+++

## PART THREE : MARGARET MARY COMING HOME | 1938

Three days later Bella repeated what she'd overheard between the two roughnecks and the barber. Gossiping was a favorite pastime in the Manor House, especially on rainy days, and most of their days were wet. Oregonians liked to say the rainy season lasted until the 4th of July and started again on the 5th.

Bella had been in the basement working at her lace-making frame within eavesdropping distance of Patrick's barber chair. She'd heard Lex and Cox complaining about the state of the country, how Roosevelt and the Jews are fixing to get us into another war. 'Gotta watch out for those scheming buggers,' Cox said. 'I'm not gonna go overseas to fight for some dumb kikes'."

"I don't like the sound of that. They're prejudiced against the Jews," said Margaret Mary.

"I hate to think about another war," added Bella. "My uncle got bombed with mustard gas in France and he's never been right in the head since."

"George served in the Army, too," said Margaret Mary, "but they kept him in Texas. I'm glad he wasn't sent to the trenches."

"You know what else Cox said?" interrupted Bella. She lowered her voice to imitate the men 'Let them Huns and Frogs fight it out over there, that's what I say.'"

"Maybe they really are Communists," said Margaret Mary with an audible gulp. "No, I definitely do not like the sound of that."

+++

"How much d'ya think the harmonica will get us?"

Ben heard the rough whisper just as he was about to flush the toilet. He picked up his feet, held his breath, and kept eavesdropping.

"A mouth harp like that should fetch a good price from Hank at the pawn shop." He recognized Lex's voice.

"A big jug of muscatel would sure hit the spot." That was Cox.

"So how do we get ahold of the Jew's harp? He keeps it on him, even at night."

"Here in the latrine, that's our best bet. I've been keeping an eye on the old kike. He stumbles to the can around three o'clock most mornings."

"Let's grab it then, take it off him when no one's around."

"You keep watch in the hall. If anyone else shows up, tell him to go outside. I'll wait 'til the Jew's on the john with pants around his ankles. I'll yank his britches away, grab the harmonica and we'll get outta here."

"Right. The old hymie can't holler very loud, can hardly even move. By the time he figures out what's happening, you and me are long gone."

"Goodbye harmonica, hello muscatel."

+++

"So what happened last night?" Margaret Mary's face was pink with excitement.

"Remember my request?" Ben asked. His eyes flashed beneath gray eyebrows thick as toothbrushes.

"I do. Yes, I know you don't like to be bothered when you're working, but I just couldn't wait until tonight to find out what happened with Joshua and the thugs."

She glanced at her hands, jiggling with nervous energy. She saw Ben look at them, too. Margaret Mary stiffened her spine. She knew how firmly Ben discouraged his friends from approaching his workbench during the day. He had told everyone that he was glad to chat in the evening but insisted on keeping regular business hours for customers who came from Portland with grandfather's stopped railroad watch or mother's broken heirloom pendant watch.

She grabbed one hand with the other to keep them still.

Ben took a deep breath and let out a long, resigned sigh. "All right," he said, rubbing his eyes. She could see bruised-looking circles under his eyes. It was clear he'd not had enough sleep.

"It must have been a rough night," she began.

"It was. We had to keep watch all night. Joshua didn't come to the toilet until nearly four thirty this morning." Ben sighed again, rubbing one hand across his creased forehead. "But they didn't get away with his harmonica," he assured her, "and I don't think those two roughnecks will be giving our crippled friend any more trouble."

"Oh, thank you, Mother Mary," she said, clasping both hands to her heart. The pounding in her chest was beginning to settle down.

"How did our plan work?" Margaret Mary bumped her hip against Ben's workbench like a mischievous girl.

"Your suggestion about lard was a good one. Jasper Carroll explained the whole plan so the kitchen chief could understand why we needed it. Ollie said he couldn't let us have fresh lard but he could give us a can of old bacon grease.'

"Bacon grease. Why didn't I think of that."

"It's all right, Ollie did, and it worked great. As soon as Lex followed Joshua into the men's latrine, Jasper tackled Cox. That guy may act queer but he's mighty as a lumberjack, strong enough to keep Cox down in a headlock while I smeared grease all over the floor."

"Oh, I wish I could've seen that!" she exclaimed.

"I do, too. It was quite a sight," Ben agreed. "After a bit Lex came barreling out the door, just as you imagined he would, never expecting a greasy floor. Feet slid out from under and down he went. Whacked his head and cracked something else, maybe some ribs."

Ben's grin was grand, his tone deliciously pleased.

"What happened to Cox?"

"Jasper kept him in a full nelson until I got the night watchman to rope his wrists and ankles. They kept an eye on the prisoners while I took Joshua back to the ward. The sheriff got here about six.

While we were waiting, Jasper told me he hates bullies with his whole, sore heart but he's never had to fight so hard to keep one from hurting someone else. He crossed himself left and right, and asked the Holy Mother to forgive him."

"That young man is as nice as pie," she said.

"A very tired pie," added Ben. "We both are. Sheriff took Lex and Cox into Superintendent Jackson's office first thing this morning. I wouldn't be surprised if he kicks those two bullies off the farm."

"You did a good night's work, I'd say."

"Yes, though it took a while to get Joshua calmed down. He was quite upset."

Margaret Mary reached for Ben and hugged him exuberantly, nearly crushing the small man against her extravagant bosom. She had the urge to kiss his lips, but held it in check.

# THIRTY-FIVE

☙❧

The fact is: what almost happened to Joshua Herschel is the kind of close call that holds a community in thrall. No sooner had Lex and Cox been hauled off than the rumors began. Word spread that they'd been part of a pawnshop theft ring. Pat, the Irish barber, told of walking past the loading dock where he saw Joshua standing alone, looking pale and baffled. More than that, said Pat, the old man looked "gone." He'd called Ben from his workbench in the basement and Ben had gone right away to walk Joshua back to his cot in the men's ward. Then people said Joshua was on the verge of a nervous breakdown.

"He went through quite a shock," said Mabel May. "I think we forget how hard it can be when a man's naked and..." She stopped, suddenly embarrassed.

"Victims can't help it," Alma added quickly. She wanted to show the knitters that she wasn't some delicate flower. Two pink spots gleamed on her tan cheeks.

"Poor thing," said Bella, "poor old thing."

"Does Joshua have any family to help out?" asked Tillie. Everyone looked at her, surprised by this question.

"If any of us had family who could help out, none of us would be in this spot," said Margaret Mary, louder than necessary.

Tillie's blue gingham dress had hiked up over her fleshy thighs. She tugged it down before saying "Now's the time for the Ladies Sunshine Club to go help that poor man."

Mabel May raised her eyebrows and said that would not be necessary.

"I think it's a very kind idea," Bella contradicted. Being Italian Catholic, she had never heard of the Presbyterian Ladies Sunshine Club.

"What do you have in mind?" asked Alma.

This question stumped Tillie. Everyone was quiet, waiting for her to explain.

"Joshua is resting." Margaret Mary stepped into the silence. "And Ben is with him. That seems enough to me."

She had tried being a Sunshine Lady once and it left her with a sour taste, so she wanted to change the subject.

"Let's go see the baby chicks instead."

+++

The only sign Joshua appreciated Jasper's help was the ruddiness that warmed the old man's face whenever he caught sight of the broad-shouldered youth. Expressions of bafflement passed across Joshua's brow like swallows winging across a shaft of light when he glimpsed Jasper, then lifted into thankfulness.

On the Jewish Sabbath, Jasper began to honor the old man and his harmonica by sitting in silence on the porch to hear the call of the shofar and the chants of liturgy from inside. After services were over, oh how Joshua would play. As he slid the Hohner across his mouth his body leaned one way, then the other, hands moving effortlessly. Joshua played as fast as the wind. Jasper never tired of listening.

As winter gave way to spring, Margaret Mary worried about Jasper. He seemed preoccupied. *Was he losing weight?* His eyes looked large and unfocused. He acted peevish. She sensed Jasper's deep loss but didn't know that Joshua's music activated his sorrow. Whenever the old man played traditional songs of his people, the sounds of Jewish suffering fell hard on Jasper's soul.

+++

One Sabbath evening the tall young man rubbed his face with both hands, moved down the porch stairs and walked into the dusky light. He longed for someone to love, always had. It hurt, this longing, hurt like a clenched fist at the top of his ribcage. He moved his hands to his chest and wove his fingers into a bandage to cover the wound.

Jasper turned his back to the Manor House and looked over one shoulder. If people were watching they wouldn't be able to see that he, a grown man, was caressing his own diaphragm.

Gaining the shadowy cover of the cedar grove, he felt the large, dark fist squeezing harder. The pain brought to mind Larry, his first love. Larry was a scrawny eighth-grader with dark hair flopping across his forehead. Their voices were changing that year, his and Larry's, startling them as they experimented with mutual masturbation. His groin swelled at the memory. He moved his hand to his undershorts and imagined how it had been when his balls had still been safely tucked inside his trousers. He remembered the exquisite sensations he had enjoyed so often and so much. Mourned the loss. Ached for it.

Something in his gut knotted up. His windpipe felt tight. Jasper moved his hand away from his scarred groin, shifting his legs. There were tears on his face. He wanted to walk away from here, to keep walking until he couldn't walk any more, but he was afraid of the dark.

His heart pounded.

He slumped against a tree, slid to the ground and wept.

The rain had stopped but the earth was wet.
There were no stars.

+++

Henry Bellows, the bearded boot-maker, joined them on the porch one mild April evening. His face, as always, was as stony as Rooster Rock. When he moved around the circle giving big-pawed handshakes to everyone, Margaret Mary noticed drops of sweat at his hairline. For someone big enough to walk in and throw his weight around, Henry did just the opposite. She thought there was something touching about this.

"Henry, what's your opinion of FDR's New Deal?" asked Cracker Jack. As the most outgoing man in the group, Jack showed his welcome for the shy guy by trying to get him into a conversation.

There was no answer. Nobody expected one.

Someone mentioned the weather then things went quiet.

Henry rose, mumbled into his beard and left.

"If he's not talkative, his father probably wasn't either," said Joshua. "I never knew my father but you hardly ever heard a word out of my Uncle Sol."

+++

A few days later she said hello as she passed Henry in the Manor House. He thrust his head forward, down slightly to one side, and looked past her. She found this habit of his odd, but it never crossed her mind that Henry had been pining for her since the day he'd met her. She couldn't have imagined he'd been jealous of Ben since the first time he'd spotted them together. She knew that not everyone liked him, though. Ben thought Henry acted like he was hiding something.

"Tell me about yourself," said Margaret Mary. She could be impulsive. "Do you come from around here?"

Henry looked away, startled. He couldn't recall anyone ever asking that. He didn't know what to tell.

"Do you have any sisters or brothers?"

"An older sister, Eva."

"Do you see her often?"

"No." Henry looked at Margaret Mary from under veined lids, brown eyes wide, as though something painful had surprised him.

"Does she live far away?"

"She died."

"Oh, Henry."

To say his name like that, the way Eva had said it, choked him up. He rubbed one wrist. Curls of black hair sprang from the backs of his fingers.

"I am so sorry, Henry."

"She was sick for too long."

He had to wait a moment. She saw moisture in his eyes.

"Oh, that is sad."

"Eva's feet were always cold. I was making boots for her, lining them with red flannel when..." Henry rubbed his nose with the back of his hairy hand. Margaret Mary nodded.

"Hiram, her husband, drove up to my shop in the middle of the afternoon and I knew."

She nodded again. "Awful, wasn't it."

He shook his large head like a blinded bear. "I never finished the boots. Couldn't."

"At least she's not suffering."

Henry shifted, his boots scraping the floor. "She'd suffered too long." His voice faded.

"It's hard to see someone you love suffering."

"Eva was a good woman."

His voice returned to its normal softness.

"And you're a good man, Henry."

Hers sounded unnaturally cheery.

He gazed at her for a moment.

"I don't think so," he said.

She saw a spasm cross his face before Henry turned and walked away.

His heels thudded like anchors.

# THIRTY-SIX

☙❦

Nobody in the Manor House was surprised when the 17th of April dawned drizzly.

"Sunrise has been cancelled again," Lily White announced to women in the ward. "Cancelled like it has been most Easter mornings since I've lived in Oregon, but the sunrise service will go on as planned. Who wants to join me at the top of the knoll?"

"Who's leading the worship?" Margaret Mary asked sleepily.

"Pastor Baker, from Bessie's church. Better get moving, women. Singers from the Gospel Choir are already trudging up the hill."

Nobody expected Hazel Parker to attend the sunrise service since she was still recovering from breast surgery. "Take 'em both off," she'd told the county surgeon.

"But the cancer is only in one," cautioned the doctor.

"That doesn't matter," she'd insisted. "I've been hauling these two pigs around for my whole life and they've weighed me down long enough. Take 'em off, slice 'em up and make 'em into bacon."

Hazel enjoyed the shock on folks' faces when she said that. Most of all, she celebrated being rid of her two big breasts - heavy as hogs - and the backaches they'd caused her since girlhood.

+++

Skies were gray, but spirits were bright around the Poor Farm during that Easter season. If Margaret Mary had been able to gaze into the secret thoughts of inmates and staff, she would have discovered a whole host of gratitudes.

Lily White gave thanks for her two new physical therapy assistants, women who'd recovered from their maladies and come back to the infirmary to help others. She'd discovered the power of recruitment by quoting Ralph Waldo Emerson while she was getting people back on their feet.

"What IS rich?" Lily would ask during exercise times. "Are you rich enough to help somebody else?"

Joshua's mouth felt good again. Once he'd confessed to Dr. Furst that he had not one, but two aching molars, the Medical Director arranged for dental students from Oregon State College to pull them. Joshua soothed the empty spots with his tongue and played Hassidic wedding songs to convey his happy mood.

Marigold, who had warmed Rhoda's cancer-ridden legs until she died, was now known around the infirmary as DocCalico. The feline decided which patients to favor with her attention. She went to whoever was most in need of comfort. Folks figured the cat must take care of her own business when no one was looking because DocCalico was never seen to leave a dying patient until the final breath. Everyone agreed that the tortoiseshell formerly known as Marigold was a healing presence in the infirmary.

Superintendent BB Jackson was relieved that a Poor Farm sit-down strike had been averted. He had lost many hours of sleep worrying how to feed the old folks if the young ones stopped working in fields and barns and kitchens. Now that the economy was picking up and some of the inmates were going back to work in factories, Mr. Jackson's biggest challenge was maintaining a steady, capable labor force. Field laborers, cannery workers and meat-packers were constantly coming and going from Edgefield.

PART THREE : MARGARET MARY COMING HOME | 1938

During the Easter season, though, it was intimate matters that made Mr. BB Jackson swell with gratitude. After Mrs. Doris Jackson had heard one too many complaints about what a disappointing daughter she was, she'd departed from the home of her whining mother. Doris was glad to return to her husband, so glad, in fact, that she caressed him as she had on their honeymoon. Their exuberant marital reunion restored BB Jackson's sense of manliness and erased his yearnings for Miss Lizzie DeLuca.

Benjamin Borden's conscience felt as light as a bird on the wing. The story of his confession had gotten around but instead of feeling judged by others, he found himself basking in the warmth of acceptance. Someone had even left a note on his cot. It was in Old Testament King James language, words from Book of Daniel, Chapter Ten, Verse Nineteen.

He didn't recognize the handwriting and it was unsigned, but Ben regarded the note as an Easter blessing. He carried it in his shirt pocket and read it many times a day.

The note said "Do not be afraid, for you are deeply loved by God. Be at peace; take heart, be strong."

# THIRTY-SEVEN

൚൙

When one gets old dramatic changes can occur without warning. One day you're chugging along as usual, the next day you're flat in bed. One day you're enjoying your friends, the next you're wondering how your grandchildren will make their way in this hard world.

Thinking about her namesake Margaret, she fretted *will you get trapped in a troubled marriage?*

Thinking about Virginia Dee, she worried *will you feel abandoned by your husband?*

Thinking about Jim, she fussed *will you lose your job and your sense of purpose?*

One day you're worrying, the next day you're coughing.

+++

*Unnnhhh, unnnhhh...*

She'd been too sick with pneumonia to pay attention to much of anything except her own aches and sweats, chills and coughs. She was sleeping heavily when the moaning began. It confused her at first, made her wonder if she was the one making such primal sounds. But she wasn't. Weak daylight washed into the ward. It must be morning. *Where is the nurse, anyway?*

*Unnnhh, unnnhh...* Desolate groans rose from the mouth of a woman in the next cot.

*Sounds like someone's dying.*

Last evening Margaret Mary had caught a glimpse of a tiny form when a male orderly lifted her from the gurney. The woman might be young, perhaps Oriental, but she couldn't be sure because her face was covered with a sheet. For a while she tried to ignore the forlorn noises by pulling a pillow over her ears, but duck feathers did not block the woe.

UNNNHHH, UNNNHHH.

As the volume went up, other patients stirred awake. A few grumbled. She waited for someone bold enough to say "Hush up that noise," but nobody did. She considered saying it herself, but that didn't seem right. The groans began to take on a rhythmic pattern. Could she be chanting in Chinese?

To her great surprise, Margaret Mary found herself moaning along. *Unnnhhh, unnnhhh* she repeated in a low tone. To her even greater surprise, the small woman lowered her volume to match. She glanced over to catch the woman's eye, but her face was covered, her small form curled into a tight ball.

Let's try that again.

*Unnnhhh, unnnhhh* she groaned, increasing the loudness of her own voice.

*Unnnhhh, unnnhhh* her neighbor moaned more loudly in response. As they went on in this way, others began to chime in.

Bessie Armstrong, the ward nurse, squeaked to a halt at the door. Her hands were filled with supplies, her mind busy with tasks to do. What was this? It was startling to hear folks groaning in mutual misery. On her shift, the indigent patients usually suffered in silence.

Nurse Bessie had grown up hearing the laments of her people vocalized in work songs and church hymns. She herself began singing in the Grace Gospel Church Choir when she was half-grown. But she had never heard infirmary patients sing or moan together. Surprised as she was by the unexpected commotion, Bessie recognized an ancient truth in the way these bedridden patients were joining their voices. *Unnnhhh, unnnhhh* they sang, sometimes accidentally harmonizing. These were different lyrics from the Negro spirituals her mama and aunties sang, but the same spirit. Instinctively, Nurse Bessie joined in. She lent her soprano voice to the spontaneous and repetitive unnnhhhs of the patients. After a bit she began introducing the words of a traditional hymn ...

*Swing low, sweet chariot, coming for to carry me home...*

As unspeakable woes found voice among patients, their voices lifted in soulful harmonies, spilling the old hymn out of the infirmary and rippling down the hallway. Workers and ambulatory inmates, attracted by the beauty of song, stepped inside the ward and hummed along. Others clustered in the hall and listened with faces alight. Two Negro women reverently lifted their hands as well as their rich alto voices. Faces transformed as voices soared, a sweet, sad solace for singers and listeners alike.

As the hymn began to wind down, Margaret Mary studied the slight woman in the next cot. The patient did not uncover her face, nor did she sing the Negro spiritual, but she did unfold her origami frame from its tight fetal position.

Something is relaxing in me, too, Margaret Mary realized. All this moaning and singing must be good for the soul. She pondered this as the nurse bustled around humming *"Swing, Low"* while tending to bedridden patients. Everyone greeted Bessie with a smile this morning. Quick grins flashed between folks who had kept their sorrows to themselves until now.

Margaret Mary felt more awake than she had in a long time. The hard coughs that had wracked her chest were easing up. Only one bout of coughing interrupted her morning mush and tea. Her sense of curiosity began to reawaken, too. There is something mysterious about this tiny woman, fragile as a china doll. Whether she knows it or not, I do believe she's bringing something we need. And I bet she has a story to tell. I hope I can get her to talk.

+++

Pale light filtered through the window.
Margaret Mary cast her eyes toward the next cot.
The delicate woman pushed up into a sitting position.
They exchanged names and small pleasantries while washing their faces.
"What do you have there?" Margaret Mary asked, pointing toward a small tin can on her neighbor's lap.
"This I cannot leave behind," said Sachiko, holding up a jade-green tea canister painted with blue flowers. Gold vines twined around a red dragon.
Margaret Mary put out a hand to take it but the tiny woman quickly yanked the container out of reach. *Ooops, I mustn't be so eager.*
"These are my mother's bones," she whispered. "The red dragon guards her spirit."
Margaret Mary tried not to look as startled as she felt.
"Tell me about it," she said in a choked voice, coughing to cover her shock.
"I brought my mother's ashes from Japan after the big man found us. He brought my sister and me to this land." Sachiko stopped. An expression crossed her face that Margaret Mary could not read.
"What man was that?" She smiled encouragingly.
The shy woman cradled her mother's remains to her heart, then glanced up. Margaret Mary quickly cast her eyes away, having noticed that Sachiko clammed up whenever someone looked directly at her. "He was a sea captain, an American. Captain Mullen found my sister and me on the street in Tokyo."

"On the street by yourselves?"

"Yes, our home burned soon after Mother died. We had no place to go. We were weeping with fright." Sachiko paused again. This time Margaret Mary held her tongue.

"His big arms went around both of us at once," she went on. "Keiko was twelve year old, I was fourteen. The big American smelled of sweat and onions but seemed a decent man. He said he would take good care of Keiko and me...."

During another long pause Margaret Mary resisted the temptation to look at Sachiko's face. *Her voice sounds young but her face looks old. What does this mean?* She noticed herself softening, feeling a little more patient and a lot more protective than she had ever felt toward a foreigner.

Sachiko spoke hesitantly. "Captain Mullen took us to the harbor in a rickshaw. Everything we owned was wrapped in two cloth bundles. I carried Mother's bones on my lap." The speaker fell silent, wrapped in memories. The listener kept still, too, although she was vibrating with curiosity. She waited quietly because she sensed that Sachiko had secrets, things she didn't want others to overhear. She might turn away and cover her face at any moment.

Sachiko reminds me of a yellow finch with a broken wing, thought Margaret Mary. Her hands, her eyelids, her words, they all flutter like a flock of songbirds, sometimes breaking apart and winging in different directions. She remembered how she'd learned to wait near the bird feeder in her back yard. She closed her eyes lightly until another bit of the wild bird's tale was ready to come forth from Sachiko.

Curiosity got the better of her before long. "What happened?" she prompted. "How did you get to Oregon?"

"A very terrible journey," began the wan woman. "Captain Mullen hid us in the bottom of the ship. .... Keiko and I did not see the sun for many weeks. .... Our skin turned to salt. ... Our clothes turned to rags. ... "

She was spellbound. She had never listened to an Oriental person before and here she was, learning to listen in Japanese. George had always steered her away from pig-tailed men on the streets of Portland, men wearing wide pants and clopping along on wooden-soled sandals. Her husband had ugly terms for their kind but she booted those nasty words out of her head.

She fixed her gaze on the sick woman in the next bed. Sachiko looked tormented and Margaret Mary wanted to know why. But curiosity killed the cat, she reminded herself. And I don't want to kill Sachiko's trust in me. She bit her tongue and bided her time. Sachiko's story is hard to follow, but worth the effort, she thought. Perhaps she has no English words for what she's been through.

Slowly Sachiko went on. "Our mother's bones rattled during the long voyage. She scolded me for being so stupid, for putting Keiko in danger with a bushy-bearded stranger."

Margaret Mary listened patiently, even when whole paragraphs came out in Japanese. She concentrated fully, listening between the lines, trying to absorb the woman's meaning in a tale told in a foreign tongue.

After a while, Sachiko closed her eyes and began moaning again. *Unnnhhh, unnnhhh* she groaned. This is a language everyone understands, thought Margaret Mary. No translation needed. And I need to groan along. *Unnnhhh* responded Margaret Mary. Her eyes remained open, watchful. A line from the Twenty-Third Psalm popped into her mind, *in the valley of the shadow of death*. That's it, she realized. Sachiko needs company as she walks through the valley of the shadow of death. The two women communed softly in the ancient language of travail until Sachiko fell into a fitful sleep.

+++

Late in the day, the origami-bent woman began speaking again. Her voice was dim, as if it came from a dark and distant place.

"No air below deck. We are dying without air. Keiko and I feel so afraid when a man opens the hatch and stares down at us. The light hurts our eyes. What will he do to us. We hold each other tight, but then he hands down a tin bowl. It was some kind of mash. How we long for a bit of rice or a cup of tea but get only mashed cabbage, stale water."

"I am so sorry that happened to you," she whispered.

"It got worse when the slop bucket overflowed. The deck was so smelly and slippery we could not stand on it."

"Oh, that sounds dreadful."

"Keiko and I stayed in our bunk, too weak to walk."

"How long were you at sea?" Margaret Mary prompted after another long silence. She had never been on an ocean voyage herself and was eager to hear about Sachiko's.

"I not know. It was dark in ship's belly, always dark. Maybe nine months. I weak as a baby when we finally came to land."

"Where did you live in Portland?" Margaret Mary whispered, suddenly afraid that she might not be able to bear the answer.

*Unnnnhhh, unnnnhhhh.* Sachiko's groans were her only reply. Her anguish gushed from deep in her gut and reverberated in Margaret Mary's belly. She felt something twisting inside her, a kind of hurt unfamiliar to a chaste Catholic woman.

+++

Over the next few days, the infirmary became a sort of Scherezade chamber for Margaret Mary. She wanted a thousand and one stories, a new story every night, but she did not get one. She kept watch over Sachiko but the Japanese woman kept her face covered and kept her secrets to herself.

One blustery night she rose up with a shuddering cry. Margaret Mary startled awake to hear Sachiko blurt "The House of the Rising Sun...That's what they call the place." Her voice was harsh and hot, like charred wood after a wildfire.

"Captain Mullen took Keiko and me to ... a place of sin."

Margaret Mary watched Sachiko's face twist into something too awful to comprehend then shut her eyes in an effort to erase the dreadful sight.

As Sachiko fell into silence, Margaret Mary's heart rose into prayer. "Mother Mary," she whispered, "wrap this woman in your blue cloak of mercy. Protect her with your prayers. Heal her with your love forever and ever. Amen."

+++

The next morning DocCalico hopped onto Sachiko's bed and curled near her heart. Nurse Bessie also drew near, sensing that the tiny patient was making her final voyage. In a tender voice she began to sing .... *swing low, sweet chariot, coming for to carry me home...* Others joined in as they were able .... *swing low, sweet chariot, coming for to carry me home...*

Singing had become the way Poor Farm folks accompanied each other across the final threshold. That's how I want to go, too, thought Margaret Mary, whenever my time comes.

+++

Whatever shameful secrets scarred Sachiko's body and seared her mind, she took them to her grave that day. "A place of sin." Those were her last words.

As long as she lived, Margaret Mary would never forget Sachiko, never be able to get those anguished words out of her mind. Nor would she forgive the American sea captain who had lured two innocent Japanese girls into unspeakable lives of ruin.

But she didn't have long to live.

Heart trouble, said Dr. Furst.

# THIRTY-EIGHT

ଓଽଠ

"What's troubling your heart today, dear one?" Ben scooted a wooden chair close to her bed and brushed the hair back from her forehead. Her face was flushed, her brow furrowed.

"Albert," she said.

Ben nodded. He'd heard stories about her son and knew his friend's heartache was linked to the boy's hurtful ways.

"Tell me." His voice was soft. "Get it off your chest."

Ben enfolded Margaret Mary's hand in his two small, cool ones. Hers were jittery.

"Before the sheriff in Montana caught up with him, none of us knew the awful things my son was doing. Only one little friend, a boy called Slugger." She shook her head.

"What sorts of things?"

"Hurting dogs." She turned away from Ben, couldn't meet his eyes.

"Hurting whose dogs?"

"The neighbors. Mrs. Ellison's Sheltie."

"How did you find out about this?"

"Sheriff Bowen came to the house and asked Albert if he had done it. He grinned and told us all the details."

"What did he do?"

"Tortured the Sheltie with a knife then cut out its entrails. Leo heard the dog's screams and ran into the woods to stop it, but he was too late."

She tugged her hand out of Ben's and placed both hands over her heart. He waited until her coughing spell had run its course.

"It hurts, doesn't it?" he asked after a time.

"Yes," she nodded. "But that's not the worst of it."

"Oh. Is there more?"

She nodded, flushing a dark magenta. The color of her face alarmed him.

Ben looked around for Nurse Bessie. She wasn't in sight so he went to the sink and ran cold water over a washcloth. Wringing it out, he placed the cool cloth over Margaret Mary's forehead. She nodded her thanks and reached for his hand.

"Want to hear the worst of it?"

"Yes, my dear."

"Albert got us run out of town. We found out that my boy had been torturing and killing dogs for a long time."

"How old was he when this happened?"

"Ten. Sheriff Bowen gave us a choice. Either he would arrest Albert and send him to a home for wayward boys or the family could leave Billings."

"So you left."

"George thought we could straighten him out. I wasn't sure, but I didn't want to give up on the boy. So yes, we packed up, took the train to Portland and started over."

"Have you ever been back to Montana?"

"No."

"Not even to see your brother?"

"No, James and I have never been close."

"Couldn't you have sent Albert to live on your brother's ranch?"

"No, it was too embarrassing to tell him what the boy had done. Not that James would have taken him even if I had asked."

"Why not?"

"James and I didn't get along when we were kids and haven't paid much attention to each other since."

"How do you see it now, being forced to move to Oregon?"

"For a long time I felt lost. All I wanted to do was go home again."

"Did Portland ever feel like home?"

"Yes, once I could see God moving in his famous mysterious way. As He had been all along."

"Was God moving in his famous mysterious way to get you to Edgefield, too?"

"Yes, dear Ben. I felt quite lost here for a long while. Until I found you."

"And Bella and Joshua?"

"And Mabel May and Florrie and Buster."

"And Cracker Jack?"

"Yes, and Peppermint Tillie."

"Here in the infirmary now, are you feeling lost or found?"

"This has become my home and it's a good one."

"Knowledge of what you love comes to you, doesn't it. Seeps into you."

"Yes, I've been found, home at last."

"Anything I can do now?"

"Ask Tillie and Jack to come and sing. I want to hear that lonesome valley song."

# THIRTY-NINE

☙❧

Shivering with a sense of something just out of reach, something powerful and compelling, Margaret Mary teetered on the edge of mystery. In the dream-lit dark on the morning of her sixty-ninth birthday, she felt the weight of her mother's mother sitting on the edge of the bed. She knew who it was by the waxy feel of Granny Brigid's hand on her own, and the smoky smell of the old lady's hair.

"The saints danced the night you was born, girl!" Granny exclaimed. "Yes, they did a little jig on November the first, and wasn't that All Saints Day indeed. I was there to see it with me own two eyes."

This startled Margaret Mary. She was awake now, tuning both ears to the voice of her dead grandmother.

"Yer dear mother sailed for America with young James Doig soon after they was wed, and how I did miss her. When it came time for my sweet Phoebe to deliver you, I sensed it in me own womb. It tore my heart to not be by her side in the birthing time, but I kept a'prayin. The night you was born – 1869, it was – I stayed on me knees at St. Brendan's. All through the night I kept a'lighting candles, praying to the Blessed Mother to keep me dear lassies safe."

The burrs of excitement in Grandmother's Scottish voice delighted her. She listened with all her heart, thrilled to hear the story of her own beginnings.

'Twas late in the night," Granny Brigid recalled, "and I'd laid me old head on the plank bench fer a wee bit when something woke me up with a start. I blinked me old eyes to see the strangest thing a'happenin'. Them plaster saints in their little niches was a'movin their feet. I swear it, girl. When them sober saints started a'dancin' the Scottish jig I knew you'da come into this world in a blaze a glory!"

She remembered having heard this wild tale from her mother Phoebe, but never knew whether to believe it or not. Her mother had been old at the time, and shaky with the palsy.

She liked the vision of saints dancing on her birthday. DocCalico must've, too, because the cat hopped onto the bed and curled up on her chest. Woman and cat laid together for a long while after Grandmother's visitation faded. She found it comforting to hear Nurse Rachel softly humming as she moved between the beds, chanting an ancient night prayer in Hebrew.

... *Sh'ma... Sh'ma... Sh'ma.*

+++

After a while, an image of St. Brendan's formed in Margaret Mary's mind, a chunky little stone church on the rise of a hill. Green fields and grazing sheep spread out around the church like skirts from the hips of a maiden.

*Saint Brendan...what is it about Saint Brendan?* Soon an astonishing connection came to her. She remembered hearing about St. Brendan in catechism class. Known as The Voyager, he sailed from Ireland with brother monks to England and Scotland, then on to the Blessed Isles, as North America was known then. She even remembered the year, 575 AD.

## PART THREE : MARGARET MARY COMING HOME | 1938

*What if Saint Brendan's voyage brought him to Boston harbor centuries before my parents did? What if he blessed the place in Ontario where I was born?*

Fever and excitement fired up her imagination.

*What if The Voyager's spirit blessed my newly wed parents?*

*What if Saint Brendan himself gave them the courage to make their way from Scotland to The Land of Promise in Canada?*

Her thoughts had never gone in this direction before and now she wondered why not. Suddenly her connection with The Voyager seemed obvious and natural. *I always longed to travel,* she reminded herself, *just like St. Brendan. But after my dear dad died so young and left mama and me as poor as church mice, I never had the money to go exploring.*

*Except once.*

The enormity of the choice she'd made half a century ago fell upon Margaret Mary's conscience with the weight of a collapsing convent roof.

*I did make one voyage across the continent when I was a young lass. To enter the novitiate. I had expected to marry The Church and spend my life as a nun until I met George Wright. Sister Kathleen had convinced Mama that The Sisters of St. Mary needed my help at the new convent in Montana. Mama finally relented. She sold Papa's gold watch and chain to pay my train fare west. It was her only treasure, and she gave it all to me. And look how I squandered my mother's legacy.*

Guilt clogged Margaret Mary's throat.

Blessed Mother, forgive me, she prayed, for I have sinned.

As tears of remorse slid into her ears, the sorrowful woman slid toward sleep to the mysterious sounds of Nurse Rachel softly chanting *Sh'ma... Sh'ma... Sh'ma.*

+++

Joshua sat beside her and played his harmonica as she slipped in and out of sleep. His music made her want to kneel down, to go down on her hands and knees, to smell the good earth. It made her feel lucky to have had what she'd found here. It made her think about happily ever after.

*What is ever after, exactly?*
*It doesn't mean being happy forever, does it?*
*Is it all of our lives, our loves, our losses, all of it?*
*Is it this music floating all around?*
*Is it the blank space that goes on without us?*
*The forever after we're gone?*

+++

During the night, strange visions rose and receded in her mind like Pacific tides. They cast her ashore totally spent yet strangely willing to endure the next wave. *Are my old sins washed overboard at high tide?* she wondered.

The turbulence brought waves of grace that swept her sorrows away. Ancient angers were cast onto the shore like driftwood. She felt her soul lifted high on a tidal wave of mercy. By morning, her body was at rest. The pounding of her heart had slowed to a peaceful pace.

DocCalico noted these changes and moved on to someone more in need of feline comfort.

+++

During the day she talked nonstop about her visitors from the other world. To Nurse Bessie, to Ben, to Bella, to anyone who could listen, she described how she had died and gone to heaven, how she had come to life again.

How she had found the ancient note revealing the secret of her beginnings.

How she'd been given the key to a mystery, a rusty key that she'd lost long ago.

She had not walked into the Light.

She had not seen Jesus.

The only way she could explain it was to say she'd been suspended in a timeless past that held the key to... something.

She'd felt Granny's touch.

She'd received Mother's forgiveness.

She was no longer afraid to die.

She trusted that after she died she'd be given answers to questions she couldn't even put into words during this life.

+++

On November first, late in the afternoon her son and daughter-in-law arrived with granddaughter Margaret to pay a birthday visit. Nurse Bessie told them the old woman was very fragile. She encouraged them to keep it brief.

The patient was too weak to speak and could barely keep her eyes open yet seemed determined to see her loved ones one more time. She smiled faintly when Margaret said "I hope you get better soon."

Nurse Bessie watched them hurry away and thought they seemed relieved to go. They moved like folks who had done their duty. Perhaps they sensed death hovering nearby and didn't want to face it. Who would?

# FORTY

༺༻

"Teach me that prayer," she whispered late one night as Rachel paused beside her bed. The patient's voice was weak.

The nurse pulled up a chair and enfolded a limp hand in her two strong ones.

"The Hebrew word *Sh'ma* means listen," she began. "After Grandfather heard that I had almost drowned at Blue Lake and that *Sh'ma* was on my lips when I came back to life, he taught me about it."

Margaret Mary nodded "please go on." Rachel did.

"Grandfather told me why *Sh'ma* is so powerful. Our Jewish faith is about listening, not believing. The ears - not the mind - are the spiritual focus of my people. For me," whispered Rachel, "prayerfulness is more about listening than speaking. I pray to hear from the heart - *lev shomea*. When I listen, my whole life becomes a voice of God."

The patient squeezed her hand. Nurse Rachel continued.

"*Sh'ma* is made up of three mother sounds. The first one, *shin*, is the sound of cacophony. Would you like to try it with me, Mrs. Wright?"

Softly, without opening her eyes, the patient did. They made the sound *shin* together, repeating it quietly so as to not disturb the sleeping patients.

"*Mem* is the harmony of all sound," Rachel went on after a while. "Grandfather chanted it on a bass note, like this." She attempted to deepen her voice but it made her cough. She laughed softly then intoned the *mem* sound in her natural soprano voice.

"And *ayin*," she concluded, "*ayin* is the silence that contains all sound. Let's chant that together now." Nurse and patient joined voices, whispering *ayin* until time and sound dissolved into sacred stillness.

Enfolded in Presence, Rachel stayed near. DocCalico jumped into her lap and purred as she softly chanted in Hebrew. *Sh'ma Yisrael Adonai Eloheynu Adonai Echad.*

Eventually Mrs. Wright slipped into a deep sleep.

Sensing she was not long for this world, Rachel sent someone to get Benjamin Borden.

+++

Margaret Mary chugged along toward death like a train on rough rails, following its black cinders along the track of her years. Feeling her babies tugging milk from her breasts. Moving away from Albert's poor dead fists. Tasting the rusty blood from pulled wisdom teeth. Hearing George call to her in the long whistle of the train.

Shoes heavy with mud at her mother's grave, she thought *I have to stand here a long time if I want to learn about heaven.* She felt her heavy hips drop to earth. *The ground my mother is buried in, this is where I die.*

Ben kept vigil with his friend, recalling what she'd confided about being touched by Jesus after Molly Malone's death. He didn't expect a profound religious experience for himself. It was enough to simply sit with Margaret Mary, to keep her company as her breath grew raspy and uneven. DocCalico kept vigil, too, curled between the patient's chin and shoulder.

+++

PART THREE : MARGARET MARY COMING HOME | 1938

Early on the morning of November fourteenth Bessie Armstrong followed an inner nudge and arrived early at work. She sensed Mrs. Wright's end was near.

Bessie sent the women's ward clerk to get Bella Monelli, Tillie Akins and Mabel May Wood. Ben went to the men's ward to fetch Jack Brown, Jasper Carroll and Joshua Herschel.

Everyone came quickly, sleepy-eyed and solemn. Her favorite Edgefielders gathered around the bed.

"She's ready," said Rachel in a hush.

"Ready to be with Mother Mary and Jesus and all the saints," agreed Bessie.

Nurses and friends took hands in a circle around Margaret Mary's bedside and joined voices.

*Swing low, sweet chariot, comin' for to carry me home....*
*I looked over Jordan and what did I see,*
*comin' for to carry me home...*
*a band of angels coming to me,*
*comin' for to carry me home...*
*if you get there before I do... tell em that I'm comin' too...*
*comin' for to carry me home..*

+++

At six fifteen on the morning of November 14, 1938 Margaret Mary Doig Wright breathed her last.

She was on her way home, carried to her journey's end on the voices of one Baptist widower, one Pentecostal Negro nurse, one Jewish Anglo nurse, one Italian Catholic immigrant, one evangelical Negro knitter, one Jewish harmonica player, one Irish Catholic homosexual and one black disabled veteran with no religious affiliation. A few sleepy infirmary patients of varied races and religions also joined the chorus, a band of angels coming for to carry her home.

Before her skin cooled Ben tenderly planted a kiss on Margaret Mary's forehead.

Mabel May did the same.

Bella fervently crossed herself, blew her nose then crossed her deceased friend.

Jasper lifted his pink rosary to his lips, stepped forward and touched it to Margaret Mary's stilled heart.

When Nurse Rachel reverently pulled up the sheet to cover her face, Joshua pulled out his harmonica and blew a traditional dirge for the dead.

Jack and Tillie hummed along.

# FORTY-ONE

☙❧

The feelings of loss and sadness, peace and shalom, flickered among them the next day as Margaret Mary's friends limped and wheeled toward the cedar grove. They gathered for an impromptu memorial service, huddling close together to shield each other from the chill.

"Let's get going before the storm lets loose," Ben prompted. "Ready, Joshua?"

The twisted Jewish man nodded, dug his prized Hohner from a torn pocket and lit into a complex version of an old Christian hymn.

"Wasn't that *Amazing Grace*?" Ben asked as the last notes rode high on the wind.

"Yes, I learned it just for her," Joshua said with a shy smile. "It seemed fitting to send Miss Margaret Mary off with a tune from her own religion."

Cracker Jack spoke next. "I am rolling a cigarette in her memory. I'm not a religious man. I only pray in smoke," he said, coughing into the crook of his elbow. "She told me they burn incense in churches, that's how Catholics send up their hopes - so - I been practicing this."

He paused, inhaled a mouthful and blew one perfect smoke ring. The circle of friends watched as his ring of Camel smoke formed, lifted intact then dissipated in the cold air.

"Miss Margaret Mary, may you rise to heaven in a circle of love," Cracker Jack intoned. His resonant voice cracked on the word love. Everyone shifted.

Ben glanced at faces around the circle. It seemed to him this odd bunch felt pleased to be celebrating Margaret Mary's life in ways most fitting to each.

"The Baptists would be a more mirthful bunch if they did funerals this way," said Ben with a big grin.

"Amen, brother," called out Mabel May, echoed quickly by Alma.

"I am not an English-speaking person," Bella began in Italian-accented speech, "but I have the sorrows that you have. I much miss the lady." She held Margaret Mary's crucifix high for all to see, then wept loudly into a lace handkerchief.

Jasper stepped forward after a respectful silence. "A few words in memory of Miss Margaret Mary. These lines come from *Song of Myself, Stanza Six* by Walt Whitman, my favorite poet." Folks strained to hear his high voice. Jasper coughed then recited:

*"What do you think has become of the young and old men?*

*And what do you think has become of the women and children?*

*They are alive and well somewhere,*

*The smallest sprout shows there is really no death,*

*And if ever there was it led toward life, and does not wait at the end to arrest it,*

*And ceas'd the moment life appear'd.*

*All goes onward and outward, nothing collapses,*

*And to die is different from what any one supposed, and luckier."*

The long, thoughtful stillness was marked only by the keening wind. After a time, people looked toward Ben.

Not sure how he had become the official celebrant of this event, Ben nevertheless cleared his throat. "Who else would like to pay a tribute?"

PART THREE : MARGARET MARY COMING HOME | 1938

"My friend loved flowers," began Henry, ducking his mouth into his beard as if startled by the boom of his own voice. The boot maker was so shy, Ben was surprised when he'd asked to take part in Margaret Mary's memorial.

Henry gulped and plunged on. "If I was a rich man I would buy a whole truck load of yellow chrysanthemums in memory of her. I would plant them all over this farm." Henry choked up. So did everyone else.

Jack's eyes met Tillie's. They both looked at Jasper. All three cleared their throats. Jack said "We want to sing something for Margaret Mary."

"It's called *O Love That Wilt Not Let Me Go*," announced Peppermint Tillie. "The tune is called Saint Margaret, and the music was written by a man named Albert. No, not her son, but another, an Albert Pearce in England. Here are the words, something to remember her by." Jack passed around hand-copied pages. Paper and people shivered in the wind.

Tillie took a deep breath and let loose in her coppery alto. Cracker Jack came in with his melting-gold bass note and Jasper lifted into a silvery descant. Others slowly joined in, singing through tears:

*O Love that wilt not let me go, I rest my weary soul in thee;*
*I give thee back the life I owe, that in thin ocean depths its flow may richer, fuller be.*
*O Light that followest all my way, I yield my flickering torch to thee;*
*my heart restores its borrowed ray, that in thy sunshine's blaze its day*
*may brighter, fairer be.*
*O Joy that seekest me through pain,*
*I cannot close my heart to thee;*
*I trace the rainbow through the rain, and feel the promise is not vain,*
*that morn shall tearless be.*

"Beautiful," said Ben, wiping his eyes with a red bandana. "You sound like angels, singing that way. Now, I'm not sure this is a real benediction, but I want to close with some lines Margaret Mary liked, a blessing received from her family in 1936. Here goes:

*This is a new day, Lord. I don't know what it may bring, but please make me ready.*
*If I am to stand up, help me stand steadily.*
*If I am to sit still, help me sit quietly.*
*If I am to lie low, help me do it patiently.*
*And if I am to do nothing, let me do it cheerfully.*
*Amen.*

+++

The bitter November wind tore at thin clothes, prompting hugs between folks who rarely touched. After embraces that lasted longer than anyone had dared until now, the circle of friends began to dissipate. As the Edgfielders drifted toward the warmth of the Manor House, Mabel May spotted two familiar figures moving in their direction.

"Florrie!" she called out. "Buster!"

"They're late for the service," complained Tillie.

"Oh," cried Alma, "Buster is carrying the baby. He's got dear little Taffy in his arms!"

"That child looks pert as a robin," exclaimed Mabel May. "She is looking at us as if she's amazed beyond words."

"And Taffy's sweater is the same color as mine," added Cracker Jack, grinning down at his candy-pink chest. "Margaret Mary knitted me a big one just like the baby's."

The godmothers glanced around with pride. They had all noticed how everyone came dressed in the baby-soft sweaters the women had knitted from yarn donated by the church ladies.

PART THREE : MARGARET MARY COMING HOME | 1938

*No dull black funeral garb for Margaret Mary's mourners,* thought Mabel May. *Our friend's memorial service will go down in history as a celebration sweetened by candy-pink, spring-green and butter-yellow sweaters.*

PART FOUR

# EDGEFIELD

૭૩૮૦

## PAST AND PRESENT

*1868 - 2012*

# FORTY-TWO

☙❧

Oregon's historic commitment to care for indigent citizens, the Multnomah County Poor Farm and the life of my great-grandmother intersect in the visceral way of breath, blood and bones.

In 1868, a year before Margaret Mary's birth, Oregon lawmakers established the first public workhouse in Portland's West Hills "for people impoverished in consequence of bodily infirmity, idiocy, lunacy or other cause." Edgefield opened in 1911 to meet the same needs. Paupers toiled on the Poor Farm for decades, until it fell into disuse and disrepair. In 1990 the McMenamin brothers purchased the abandoned and vandalized Edgefield to establish a pub village. The Manor House where Margaret Mary spent the last four years of her life has been beautifully refurbished. Local artists adorned the doors with original paintings and covered the overhead pipes with quirky images.

Multnomah County's poorhouse was well established by the time my great-grandmother's family immigrated to Portland via Canada, South Dakota and Montana. As Margaret Mary raised her sons in North Portland I wonder if she gave any thought to the poorhouse in the West Hills where young and old derelicts lived under one roof. As George labored in the construction trade to support the family, did Margaret Mary know their tax dollars provided for lepers, addicts and tuberculosis patients all mixed together in a scene from Dickens? Did her prayers include folks who were down on their luck, dependent on the dole? Did she agree with the church ladies who declared the original workhouse deplorable and insisted on closing it down?

Did Margaret Mary cheer – or even notice - when County Commissioners bought 345 fertile acres near Troutdale and announced plans to put indigent vagrants to work in the fresh air? Did she see newspaper photos of local laborers erecting the grand four-story brick building where she would later come to heal? Did she support or oppose the government officials who invested $100,000 in 1910 dollars to build housing for paupers? Did she and George talk about any of this at the dinner table? Did she ever imagine that the new Manor House would someday become her last home?

In 1911 when construction of Edgefield was complete, inmates were transported from the old workhouse to the new Manor House near the Columbia River. There men who worked on the land planting onions, raising hogs, tending chickens and digging potatoes were fed from the "meat table." Elderly and disabled inmates unable to do manual labor ate from the "mush table."

Twenty-four years after it was dedicated, my great-grandmother became an inmate at Edgefield alongside six hundred destitute drovers, miners, carpenters and tradesmen. She lived in over-crowded conditions amongst clerks, cooks, teachers and seamstresses whose livelihoods disappeared in the depths of the Great Depression.

In 1994 McMenamin's Vintage Edgefield opened to guests who had discretionary dollars. The Manor House where Margaret Mary suffered, recovered, befriended and died has been attracting ghostly and earthly visitors ever since.

PART FOUR : EDGEFIELD PAST AND PRESENT | 1868 - 2012

Halfway House, the stone shed where Margaret Mary's sheet-covered body awaited the coroner in 1938, has been converted from a morgue into a studio called EarthArt ClayWorks. Creative clay creations now rest in the space once occupied by the corpses of paupers.

+++

I have slept in three different guest rooms in the beautifully restored Manor House, wondering which rooms might have sheltered Margaret Mary. I've savored fine foods in the Black Rabbit Restaurant, dishes seasoned with herbs grown in Edgefield's garden. I've enjoyed pizza and watched films in the pub theatre that formerly did duty as the power station. I've soaked in the free-form hot saltwater pool behind Ruby's Spa, the building that once housed resident doctors and nurses. I've attended two family weddings on the wide lawns and watched golfers play on greens that once grew grains to feed the inmates. I've quaffed Edgefield's handcrafted beer and sampled cabernet from its winery. I'm not a whiskey drinker, but fragrances rising from the distillery and restaurant kitchens now supplant the smell of adversity that marked Margaret Mary's time here.

+++

In 2012, the grandmothers gather on these pages to restore the circle of life broken by poverty. The Edgefielders' stories remind writer and reader alike that we live in two realities, material and spiritual worlds. The McMenamin brothers have done wonders on the material plane. Guests now sip handcrafted ales and wines in the delousing shed where Margaret Mary's mattress and bedding were fumigated for the next infirmary patient. The visionary brothers converted the root cellar into the Distillery. Whiskey, brandy and gin are now produced where Poor Farm cooks once stored potatoes. The infirmary wing basement has become a candlelit winery and tasting room. Guests sit at British pub tables with a view into the Tank Room where Pinot Gris wines ferment. The water tower – now empty – supports hop vines for the brewery. Who knows, perhaps the McMenamin brothers will crown the old farm silo with a bar that rotates like the Space Needle, treating guests to a 360-degree view of the gardens, vineyards and pathways below.

As much as I appreciate the enormous investment Mike and Brian McMenamin have made to restore the old Poor Farm and create a charming pub environment at Edgefield, my heart remains with the inmates. People who dwell together in close proximity can – and do - awaken the wisdom in each other's hearts. Surrendering to the guidance of ancestors from the Thirties, my mission was confirmed. It is on the spiritual plane.

As the inmates grew bolder in my imagination the Edgefielders who survived Margaret Mary insisted their stories need wider exposure than the printed page can provide. They tell me that they want to see faces from the Thirties - faces of struggle and courage - projected onto the big screen. They can imagine strangers sitting together in big, dark rooms the way folks gather in the Power Station theatre. They want a large, wide audience to experience the loves and losses, conflicts and reconciliations the original Edgefielders went through when thrown together by economic woe.

I remind these persistent and quirky folks I'm just a writer. Filmmaking is beyond my ken. They are an insistent bunch, though. They still want what they want. The Edgefielders of the Thirties tell me they want a film focused on the common humanity they discovered - and to which they contributed – as a cast of complex characters who lived together at the Multnomah County Poor Farm in Troutdale, Oregon.

PART FIVE

# JUDITH

☙❧

# SETTING OUT

*2010*

# FORTY-THREE

⊗

Setting out, I wondered how people from wildly divergent faith traditions managed to live together during the 1930s. I had more questions than answers. Many were personal.

Could I cast light into the shadows inherited from dearly beloved parents and grandparents who kept my foremother's situation a secret?

Could I reclaim the story of a woman who was treated like an outcast, the one who had become a stranger in the family?

Could I open up more breathing space in the secrecy inherited by the younger generations? I wanted to lighten the burden, if I could, for my three kids, seven nieces and nephews, six grandkids and future descendants.

Could such severe, even shocking, generational brokenness be mended?

Could a series of interconnected stories about Poor Farm residents make a difference in today's fast-paced digital world?

Would anyone want to read such tales?

And finally, was I the one to write these stories?

Did I have what it takes to write true to the soul of Margaret Mary and those with whom she shared the final four years of her life?

My family did not talk openly about religion but I heard enough disparaging remarks about Catholics when I was young to lead me to think Protestants were right and Roman Catholics were "the wrong sort." I was in my sixties by the time I discovered why my parents were anti-Catholic. Their views were rooted in choices made by one foremother, the one whose story you have just read. Margaret Mary Doig Wright held strongly to Roman Catholic beliefs and devotional practices. My family probably saw her as a symbol of the wrongdoings of a powerful religious group with which they disagreed. My hypothesis – and I could be wrong - is that my Protestant kinfolk blamed the Catholic Church for her pennilessness because she donated money to her local parish. Perhaps they couldn't acknowledge their own sense of disgrace over the fact that their foremother had fallen into poverty. Perhaps they couldn't face their own guilt about committing Grandmother to a public institution.

As I set out on the project, my hypotheses raised tough questions. Writing her story would mean taking her side. Could I do it? Could I penetrate the layers of shame, sorrow and regret embedded in the hearts and minds of the Wright family, and in myself?

The writing process did not go smoothly. First I composed tales about Margaret Mary and her peers from a third-person perspective, but the results were disappointing. After a time, I put myself in her shoes and re-wrote it in her voice, first-person. A jury of my peers judged both versions inadequate. I quit writing, figuring I wasn't good enough, doubting I had the skill to do it.

Then something odd happened. I sensed myself taken by the scruff of the neck, not by my great-grandmother herself but by a cadre of Manor House residents. A voice I did not recognize directed me to keep writing. It declared that the Poor Farm was a merciful place, that Edgefield became an interfaith community where peculiar people learned to respect and understand one another during the Depression. "The Edgefielders matter," the unknown voice insisted. "These stories matter. Don't give up. Get help. Find a coach.

You must listen when the Spirit says listen and write when the Spirit says write."

+++

Hard times were reported - quite factually - in the media during the Thirties. There was plenty of recorded information to uncover. I did plenty of research because I wanted to stay close to the historical facts but I also wanted to weave a fictional element into the tapestry of the past. Fiction was the only way I knew to emphasize four aspects that mattered to me.

First, I wanted to evoke personal details of the Great Depression from the perspective of the have-nots. It was important to describe working-class experiences of deprivation.

My second purpose was to explore personal relationships, to listen for ways people of different races and religions create community when economic necessity forces them to live in close quarters.

A third aspect was to imagine what happened internally, to explore what went on in the spiritual realm. Within the aging men and women of Edgefield I found strong moral centers. Many had an internal compass that guided them to take the high road despite impoverished circumstances.

And my fourth purpose - as a writer who was raised in a blue-collar family - was to explore how systems of economic disparity shaped hearts, minds and souls.

Touching the hem of history like this, through the imaginal realm, gives personal and spiritual meaning to large economic and political events. Until the Thirties, enterprise and daring wrote the classic novel of the United States, asserting that the national economy was too big and strong to fail. Only when the stock market crashed in 1929 and countless banks closed did Americans see the economic folly to which they had been blind. All of a sudden people looked around and said they couldn't believe this was happening. In fact, we can now see how the Depression of the 1930s was almost inevitable.

Fallout from the economic meltdown of 2008 added to my sense of urgency. The recession prompted me to buckle down. The time had come to listen inwardly, to do my best to compose *The Edgefielders: Poor Farm Tales of a Great Grandmother*.

# FORTY-FOUR

☙☙

***Place of death: Multnomah County Poor Farm***
***Date of death: November 14, 1938***

"WHAT?!" I shouted. "How could this have happened?" I rose to my feet and shook the death certificate at her. My hand felt like it was on fire. Aunt Margo raised both hands, palms out, defending her self. She looked at me as if she couldn't believe I was acting so crazy. Her stunned expression didn't stop me. I was fired up.

"How could they have sent your grandmother away!" My voice came out much louder than necessary.

"How could your father send his mother away? What gave him the right to send my great-grandmother to die in a public institution for paupers?"

What began as an ordinary visit with my elderly aunt was turning into a confrontation. An hour earlier I had arrived at Margo's house in Portland for a summer visit. Neither of us anticipated an upset. We hugged and chatted, sipped tea at her kitchen table and caught up on the news. I admired the plums ripening on a tree in her backyard and requested a jar of plum jam for Christmas. She admired the birds eating seeds from the feeder just outside her window.

+++

"Now I have some treasures to show you," she announced. I followed her into the living room and kicked off my wooden Dr. Scholl sandals to get comfortable. She kept her shoes on. Margo wasn't the barefoot type. We sat close on the maroon couch, hips and knees touching. Her legs were covered with polyester slacks. Mine were bare beyond denim shorts. The couch fabric felt scratchy against my skin. Sun beamed through the window behind us, warming our shoulders. Stacks of photocopied documents covered the coffee table.

"I've made some exciting discoveries at the Multnomah County Office of Public Records," she announced. Margo was fascinated with genealogy. I wasn't but I enjoyed her enthusiasm. She showed me addresses she had copied from hand-scribed city ledgers, lists of places her grandparents had lived since 1904 when they moved to Portland. We studied the places her parents had worked before they met and after they married.

When she held out her grandmother's death certificate I took it, as I had the other papers, and read each line. Margaret Mary Wright. Born November 1, 1869. Died November 14, 1938. Place of death: Multnomah County Poor Farm. The last line hit me like a firebomb. I felt as if I'd been handed a live grenade.

WHAT?! My voice was raw with shock, loud with protest. Multnomah County Poor Farm! I remember shouting the words. I'm usually calm and contained, but the visceral force of this news catapulted me off the couch and onto my feet. My uncharacteristic behavior startled both of us.

Margo thrust her hands out in a defensive pose, as if to protect herself. "I'm not to blame," she said in a small voice. "It wasn't my fault." Light from the window shone on her soft white hair. My aunt looked frail and frightened.

I tried to take the pepper out of my voice. "I know it's not your fault, but how could this have happened?"

"I was in college then." Her voice, usually bright, had shriveled. "Grandmother's husband left her during the Depression. She had no place to live. My parents couldn't keep her. It was the only thing they could do."

"Did you ever visit her at the Poor Farm?"

"Once, on her birthday. There was no pleasure in it, and yet I went."

"Why?"

"Visiting Grandmother was my duty. It was important to do the 'done thing.'"

"Was that the only reason you made the trip to see her?"

"No. I was her eldest granddaughter, named for her, so I wanted her to know she still mattered to me. I think I wanted assurance that I was still important to her."

"Were you?"

'No, she barely acknowledged me."

"Did that hurt your feelings?"

"Yes."

"Had you waited too long?"

"Yes, I'd waited until her birthday but it turned out to be her last. I felt awkward in the infirmary and got out as fast as I could."

"Did she say anything before you left?"

"She was too sick to talk."

"Did you say anything?"

"I said I hope you get well soon. She died a few days later."

# FORTY-FIVE

☙❧

"Dad, I'm itching to hear about you grandmother."

I greeted him exuberantly upon arrival at my dad's small house on the shore of a small lake. After driving up scenic Highway 28 and winding along narrow roads through the Mount Hood National Forest, I was eager to hear his stories.

After putting my luggage in the guest room and bringing him a Pepsi, after Dad relaxed in his recliner and I perched on a hassock nearby, I could hardly wait to focus on Margaret Mary Doig Wright. I was eager to pump him for information but first I needed to listen to his complaints. Dad had lots. He just didn't have any pep these days. This made him cranky. While he talked I tried to figure out how to approach my topic without getting his back up. I didn't want to sound like a prosecuting attorney as I'd done with Aunt Margo, so I tried to strike an encouraging tone.

"Tell me about your grandmother." I spoke gently, softly, encouragingly. "Whatever you can remember."

"I'm getting too old to remember much of anything," Dad complained, rubbing a hand across his whiskery jaw and turning to gaze out the window. I looked, too. The sky tumbled with thunderclouds, a common weather pattern during summer afternoons in the Mount Hood National Forest. Since Mom's death a decade ago, my father had been paying very close attention to the weather, noting hourly changes in temperature and barometric pressure. His moods seemed to rise and fall accordingly. If I'd been more attuned to the way he took weather changes personally, I'd have recognized the signs of an approaching storm.

"But Dad," I wheedled, "you're the only one left to ask. Your sister is the only other living person who knew Margaret Mary and she couldn't tell me much. Yesterday I was shocked when Margo showed me your grandmother's death certificate. I never knew she spent the last four years of her life at the Poor Farm. I've not heard any family stories about Margaret Mary Wright. I want to know all about her, all about how she got to Edgefield. Tell me everything!"

"Like what?" he said, shooting me a wary glance. He sounded grumpy, as usual. I sounded like a high school cheerleader.

"What she looked like, what she sounded like, what the two of you did together when you were young. Anything that will help me to know her better."

"Hold your horses, Judith! I hardly knew the woman. She spent all her time at church and she made me go with her when I was too young to know better."

"How did that happen?"

"When I was a little boy I used to stay overnight at Grandmother's house. She cooked hot wheat mush for my breakfast. I liked that, but I hated church. When I refused to go to Mass with her, she stopped inviting me to spend the night. I didn't have much to do with her after I was five or six."

"But I want to hear more…"

"That's all I can tell you." He shifted, showing his uneasiness. "I don't remember anything else about her." The conversation was over. He would not be pushed. He'd given me plenty to think about, though. More than enough.

+++

The clamor of his television was so loud I couldn't hear myself think but I needed to think about all this so I went for a walk in the forest. What was going on here? Margo and Jim both clammed up when I asked questions about their grandmother and her fate. Their memories are blank, they say. He claims amnesia. She didn't participate in the family decision but she was the sort who liked to show the family's best face to the world. Did my aunt think it reflected badly on the Wrights because her parents sent her grandmother to Edgefield? Did the decision seem ugly to her? Morally wrong? Disgraceful?

So, what do I know? Almost nothing. Either knowingly or unknowingly, my dad and aunt are leaving me with dozens of unanswered questions. I can feel myself becoming obsessed with the stranger in the family, the woman nobody wanted to talk about.

I sat on a flat rock beside the stream to ponder the dilemma. I tried to put myself back in 1934, to imagine what the Wright family had to face. Why didn't Leo and Cordelia take her in? True, there was no accessible place for Margaret Mary to sleep at their house, but did they have to send her to the Poor Farm? I wanted to believe they did the best they could, but couldn't they have acted with greater kindness? Couldn't they have explored options with her rather than deciding for her?

The fundamental question: Why didn't a family member take her in? Perhaps I suspected from the start that the answers to my big questions were not here, not to be found in the memory banks of Margaret Mary Wright's last two surviving grandchildren, but I wasn't ready to give up.

+++

"Did you think maybe your parents were being unfair to your grandmother?" I asked the next day.

"Unfair!" Dad's face twisted in scorn. "Not after what she did!"

"And what was that?"

"Gave all her money to the priests."

He was firing up. This topic was definitely a hot button

"The goddamned church took every dollar and left her without a penny to her name!"

"Maybe she didn't see the connection between her own charitable generosity and winding up as a recipient of charity."

"Not on your life! Too proud of her church," he snorted.

"It sounds like your parents decided to leave her to her own suffering, then."

"Don't say such things. You weren't there!"

His eyes blazed, showing the cynical hardness that James Leo Wright concealed from many people. My father punched the remote and turned his face to the daily stock market report. I'd been dismissed. I sat mute while the TV blared. He was nearly deaf but I wasn't. Our relationship was tense, not for the first time.

I took another walk and tried to digest the sad little story. Then I washed the Honda. It took a long time to get my thoughts in order. It took even longer to scrub off the traitorous smell of what my ancestors had done.

Over the next few days I came back to the topic from several different angles, listening for some trace of conscience or scruple from my father. Could I hear anything that hinted at a moral choice being made in 1934? So far, he'd only expressed judgment of Margaret Mary for her religiosity and blame against the Roman Catholic Church. He firmly believed it was the priests who snookered his grandmother out of her money, and he was still furious about it.

On Sunday morning I cooked his favorite breakfast, a pot of whole-wheat cereal. I topped it with brown sugar, strawberries and half-and-half. This put him in a good mood. I refilled our coffee cups and circled back to the topic on my mind.

"Why do you think your parents sent Grandmother Wright away? Was it to protect their own well-being?" I asked, trying to keep my tone level.

"You don't have any idea what it's like to live hand to mouth," he snapped. "During the Depression you had to bite and claw your way through every single day, even it meant stepping on someone else's toes. My folks didn't have a choice."

"I'm not judging you, Dad. It wasn't your fault."

"It was hard on my mother. She was a soft-hearted church lady but she had to toss her ideals out the window."

"What do you mean?"

Shooting a glare in my direction, he shot back. "You're asking too damn many questions, Judith. You've had too damn much schooling." He shook his head, as if despairing that I would ever understand.

I gave him an encouraging smile. No hard feelings.

"How about your ideals?"

Dad drained his coffee cup. Was he about to clam up and stomp off?

"I'd really like to know."

Dad didn't look at me but he did hold up his green cup. I rose to refill it and held my tongue in case he had more to say. He moved his cup in small circles to cool the coffee and stared into the depths of it. ""School was boring."

Now we were getting somewhere. I kept quiet, nodding to show I was listening.

"So I dropped out after my sophomore year and went to work. Started working at sixteen. Work was my best teacher."

I couldn't help grinning at the old rascal. He grinned back. It was good to see him feeling more relaxed.

"Tell me about the work that taught you the most."

"Investing. People always need money."

"Money's power, isn't it, Dad?"

"You bet! After what my family went through during the Depression I knew I'd never get anywhere if I spent my whole damn life driving a milk truck. So I made my own way, investing in stocks and bonds."

"And you did well at it."

"Damn right! How else was I gonna enjoy a few of the good things in life? Without investing in stocks I'd never have been able to build this house for your mother."

"You used your brains to make money."

"I had to. I was a smart boy who liked to gamble."

"Nobody could doubt that," I said with a small smile. "But couldn't you have used your smarts with more kindness and mercy? I'm thinking of your grandmother."

He gave his usual shrug. "Maybe, but I didn't try. That was my father's business, not mine. He'd been out of a job for years so I had to work my butt off every day of the Depression to keep my little sisters and brother alive. Then I met Mildred and asked her to marry me. And before long you came along."

He got a faraway look in his eyes and turned toward the window.

I wanted to say something but I had no idea what to say so I cleared the table instead. *Don't just sit there, do something useful.* I could hear my mother's motto in my mind's ear. Whenever words failed, Mom moved into action. I tend to do the same.

Dad thudded into his recliner and gazed out over the lake. The conversation was over.

Was it true Margaret Mary gave all her money to the church?

Have I unconsciously adopted my great-grandmother's pattern of excessive self-giving?

Is he warning me not to follow in her footsteps? I had to wonder...

+++

PART FIVE : JUDITH SETTING OUT | 2010

I took a long time washing the dishes, gazing through the kitchen window at his rhubarb patch. Then I studied the raspberry patch. Both were healthy and produced lots of good fruit. It dawned on me that Dad cared for his raspberries the way he had faithfully cared for his children, tilling the ground, planting and fertilizing, watering and trimming. His raspberry vines were well trained. They grew obediently along the sturdy wires he'd strung between fence posts. His raspberries went exactly where he intended. Had my brothers and I been as responsive to Dad's guidance? Probably not.

I stood at the sink meditating on the parents whose values and actions shaped my own. I wondered what my sons and daughter thought about the way I raised them. I prayed that my baby grandson was faring well under the care of his struggling parents. I pondered my grandparents who'd been forced into an impossible dilemma.

All of a sudden I felt myself at the center of seven generations. I saw an image of a teeter-totter, of myself as the fulcrum of this family.

Could my efforts to uncover hidden family truths ease things for Michael, Ray, Penelope and their cousins?

What might I discover that is worth passing on to my grandchildren and their children?

Am I being called into this writing project to help loved ones in the three younger generations avoid some of the past mistakes made by their – by our - forbears?

Questions came like stones in an avalanche. The weight fell upon me like a load of cement

+++

What can I learn from the three generations of Wrights ahead of me - Margaret Mary and George, Leo and Cordelia, Jim and

Mildred? What can I unearth that might benefit Michael, Ray, Penelope, their kids and their cousins?

What does it mean to stand at the center point of seven generations? I feel the weightiness of my position as firstborn daughter and eldest granddaughter.

I didn't know where to go with all this. It occurred to me to ask my great-grandmother for counsel but she was long gone. Standing the kitchen sink, I felt my face grow hot with embarrassment as the chorus in my head tuned up.

What a silly idea, asking a dead woman for advice.

You're a grown woman. How can you be so childish?

Then came a different voice, calmer and sweeter.

"What does Love require of you?" asked Margaret Mary.

"What does Love require?"

PART SIX

JUDITH

☙☙

THE JOURNEY

*1995-2010*

# FORTY-SIX

൞

How many women in how many stories have set out on a journey? *Find out.* The words came in a whisper, as if from the grave. *Find out.*

And isn't that the center of every story, the need to know? Doesn't it press from behind, beckoning every author forward? Of course, there are a thousand versions of the journey story. Everyone is on a journey. Truth is sleeping on the other side of what I know about myself, beyond what I can guess about Margaret Mary.

How dangerous can a tiny shred of truth be? It has neither teeth nor talons. No, if a secret is only unrealized knowledge, what harm can it do? And yet a woman has to learn what she already knows, somehow. I'm ready to have the veil taken from my eyes. Margaret Mary tells me to find out, so I need to find out.

+++

I have aged since I first learned about Margaret Mary. And here's the thing - even if I had known her personally, I'm not certain she'd want me poking into her secrets. She is so easily embarrassed, and I have so many self-doubts. I wish my great-grandmother would step out from between the beds at the infirmary and give me a hug of encouragement. She would be kind. I know that. She had a compassionate heart, wasn't one to hold a grudge. She could also be stubborn, so she'd tell me to keep writing, to stay the course. Love doesn't change, she'd say. It's not like the moon or the tides. Love is the single constant in the universe. Trust in love. So I keep listening and writing, holding my ancestors in one chamber of my heart and my descendants in the other.

+++

I am no longer young. In the winter of life, soul questions are bread-of-life to me. All six grandchildren are precious in my sight. How can I best nurture their concerns? My three adult children, too, wrestle with questions of meaning and purpose. How can I support their soul journeys? Eventually my unborn great-grandchildren will join the quest. I need to find a way to join my prayerful care with my writerly life, to do all within my power to nourish their goodness.

+++

Darkness surrounds our family history. Candlelight represents the future. I light two round, luminescent globe candles as I begin to compose stories set in Oregon during the Depression-era Thirties. These candles are gifts from my daughter. As they flicker on the desk I see one as the candle of the past. It represents the time before any of us knew each other. Its flame symbolizes the times we rested in our mother's wombs and, before that, when our mothers were in their mother's wombs.

The second candle symbolizes what is yet to come. It represents the power of hope. The energy of its flame shines on ahead, lighting the way toward connections of love that dwell in ancestral memory that moves into unknown. It symbolizes unseen possibilities.

+++

At Edgefield I stood for a moment on the porch of the Manor House and tried to prepare myself. But how can you prepare yourself for something you know nothing about? Of the woman I was seeking I knew nothing, or next to nothing. Filled with uncertainty, I put my hand on the doorknob and pulled open the door.

The entry hall was substantial. Edgefield's Manor House had become a hotel since her days as an inmate here. I saw apparent welcome in the smile and gestures of the young woman at the registration desk. Behind these I detected a certain professional courtesy.

"Would you have records on the residents who lived in this building during the 1930s?" I hoped I might find documents from the Depression here at Edgefield, although I hadn't really expected it.

"No. Nothing remains from that era," she said.

I cleared my throat nervously. "How might I find out which room my great-grandmother lived in?"

She looked at me and blinked, uncertain how to answer. "I have no idea. But good luck," she added, looking down at the desk and shuffling a stack of papers.

I'll need it, I thought.

+++

I wandered the long halls, looking for clues. There were no records of my great-grandmother's residency. Decades had passed since she lived under this roof. Major remodeling had converted the Manor House into a hotel. Local artists had been commissioned to paint vivid regional scenes on the doors of each bedroom. Fantasy creatures peeped from the overhead water pipes, even from fuse boxes on the walls. None of her personal belongings remained in this big brick building, yet I felt her presence in the woodwork. I could even sense the pattern of her lopsided gait on the wooden floorboards.

One sepia photograph attracted me. Greatly enlarged from the original, the framed photo hung on the wall of a main hallway. I stood before it for a long while, gazing at four stout ladies in a sitting room. They were seated in wicker chairs. A cane leaned against one.

I envisioned myself stepping into the picture frame,. I nodded to each of the four women then turned to one.

"Are you Margaret Mary Wright?"

In my imagination she nodded.

"I'm your great-granddaughter."

She nodded again and smiled tentatively. "I've been expecting you." Her voice was barely audible.

I picked up the cane and asked "Is this yours?"

She nodded and reached for my hand. Hers was dry and soft. Mine was shaking.

We were shy with each other. I couldn't think what to say. She gave me a clue by brushing one hand over the fabric stretched across her lap.

"Oh," I said. "Is this the cotton print dress Cordelia sewed when you got out of the infirmary?"

She nodded again. "The Magi asked her to make it for me. A gift to celebrate my return to life." Her voice was soft and reverent.

PART SEVEN

# JUDITH

✼

# COMING HOME

*2012*

# FORTY-SEVEN

୬୫୪

I prefer life to be sweet and uncomplicated. I don't like it when difficult events disturb my inner tranquility. But being stuck, unable to write, is a condition far from tranquil. I'm old enough to know that life brings certain difficulties, but not old enough to face them squarely. The work did not go quickly but was worth the effort each time I put in an honest day's words.

Composing the final section of Margaret Mary's story was particularly difficult. For some reason, I found it hard to envision how she moved through 1938, what gifts and challenges she encountered in her final year of life. Unsure what to write, I fell back on the comforting ritual of lighting a candle and waiting in stillness. I wasn't writing this section during the liturgical season of Epiphany but an epiphany struck anyway. The light revealed that Margaret Mary was as powerless to stop what would happen in 1938 as she had been in 1868 when James Doig impregnated Phoebe McCliemont Doig.

Writing about Margaret Mary's life and death turned out to be a way of cherishing her. Browsing back over the course of her years at Edgefield gave me a flood of good feelings. Things weren't always easy for her, or happy. I started this project writing from indignation and ended up writing in joy. And I discovered something about the metabolism of a writer. Just as walking aerobicizes the body and releases a flow of endorphins, the discipline of writing alters the chemical balance of the soul. Composing Margaret Mary's thoughts and actions metabolized some of the misery I had inherited. The practice of meditative writing restored me to balance and equilibrium. Even when I was out of sorts, laboring to get her story on the page gave me a sense of purpose, right action and eventually, clarity.

+++

"You're becoming kinder," said my husband. I glanced across the breakfast table. He was gazing at me tenderly, a spoonful of granola midway to his mouth. Pete's words surprised me because he does not usually converse during breakfast, preferring to quietly read the Los Angeles Times. "And you're becoming more gentle, too."

Now he had my full attention. I put down my teacup.

"Not that you weren't kind and gentle already," he added, "but lately you show more kindness and gentleness toward more people in more situations. I think it's connected to your writing. Spending time with Margaret Mary seems to be changing you for the better."

I thanked him for sharing. My beloved turned back to his newspaper. I refilled my cup with Scottish Breakfast tea and took a contemplative pause.

Cherishing is more than a mood: it is a decision. My beloved partner cites evidence that my soul has become more beneficent because of the decision to cherish my great-grandmother's soul. Spiritual growth must be built into this writerly life. Listening for and recording Margaret Mary's story not only changed me, it made me aware of how other inmates at Edgefield changed in response to each other. Writing about their strengths and frailties deepened my own sense of continuity as I became aware of the continuity among them.

Pete's spontaneous feedback recalled "the fruit of the Spirit" described in Galatians 5:22-23, one of my favorite texts. Early in seminary Rev. Glenda Hope had introduced the fruit of the Spirit as discernment tool. "Notice moments of generosity, peacefulness or patience when you're doing acts of ministry," she said. "Watch, also, for times when kindness and gentleness are absent. The fruit of the Spirit will help you discern whether or not you're on the right track."

I imagined Glenda pulling up a chair and seating herself at our breakfast table. "Does the act of writing, the decision to bring your great-grandmother from the shadows of secrecy into the light of truth, add to your joy, kindness and generosity? "It was Glenda Hope's tensile-strength voice, clear in my memory.

"Does the rigor of composing tales for hard times increase your personal faithfulness, gentleness and self-mastery?"

"Has immersing yourself in the Great Depression become a spiritual discipline, imagining how people learned to cope when they were totally down and out?"

Yes, I say. Yes.

"Can you handle three more discernment questions?" Even in memory and imagination, I found Glenda's questions as piercing as they were in the early '80s when I was a student at Pacific School of Religion.

Yes, I nod.

"Has your energy increased since you committed yourself to the ministry of writing for publication?"

Yes.

"Has your creativity deepened during the years you've spent researching, writing and revising this book?"

Yes.

"Are you experiencing a greater sense of freedom in this work than you did in earlier forms of ministry?"

Absolutely!

"There you have it," said Glenda.

# EPILOGUE

It makes me happy that Margaret Mary finally found her place in a beloved community. She came home at last, to the place she belonged. At the Poor Farm she chose friends of generosity and goodwill.

Did she choose me, too? Yes, I think so. Her spirit of love remains available to me - and to all our descendants - as we find our way forward in a world more complex than she could have imagined in 1938.

So, yes, I have changed in the course of this project. Beyond the increase in kindness and gentleness that Pete reports, I've become more willing to seek my great-grandmother's advice. During contemplative pauses I find myself consulting her spirit.

"What would you like me to know now?" I asked Margaret Mary recently. Then I sat in receptive stillness.

After a time I heard "Welcome your embarrassment."

What? First I laughed then I flushed. My face can turn hot at a moment's notice. How could a great-grandmother who died before I was born possibly know about my embarrassing tendency to blush my way through adolescence?

In my forties I turned red from the top of my skull to the center of my chest each time I preached a sermon. How could she know that? Margaret Mary never saw the high-necked robe that covered every inch of my throat and chest. She didn't know I justified the expense of a custom-made clergy robe to keep my crimson skin covered. It cost twice as much as one off the rack but my mother understood. It was her graduation gift. I wore the long white robe every Sunday until retirement. It still hangs in the closet, in case I'm asked to officiate at a wedding or funeral. I keep it because this robe was Mom's last gift to me. She died a few days before I graduated from Pacific School of Religion.

Now my great-grandmother tells me "Welcome your embarrassment."

I've always hated the way my face blazed. In middle age I grew more accustomed to sudden flares of embarrassment but told myself it was an unfortunate legacy from Scottish ancestors. My skin flushes whenever I do or say something awkward. Even the mortifying memory of a long-ago event can redden my face. To this day I even turn crimson in the stillness of Quaker Meeting whenever I sense a message rising within. Gradually I came to realize that such a flush is more than personal embarrassment. I've come to recognize it as a signal that Spirit is present and urging me to speak.

"Welcome your embarrassment," she repeated. "Embrace it," she insisted.

"Tell me more," I invited.

"Explore generosity," nudged Margaret Mary.

Okay. I turned on the computer and typed *embarrassment* and *generosity* into the search engine. Google is a resource she never could have imagined.

A quick search revealed a new study from the University of California, Berkeley linking embarrassment and generosity. To measure embarrassment, researchers asked participants how they'd feel in awkward situations and recorded their responses. Then subjects were directed to play a game that measured their willingness to share personal resources.

The results? Easily abashed persons are more generous and most willing to cooperate with others. Pink-faced folks demonstrate a higher-than-usual tendency to communicate to others. Respondents did not view easily embarrassed people as being weaker or more vulnerable. That's a relief. The research team concluded that blushers value social relationships and are more likely than non-blushers to share what we have with others.

Long after her earthly life Margaret Mary Wright is still gifting me, this time with self-acceptance. She asked me to pass on permission to blush so here it is. Great-grandmother gets the last word. It's okay to turn red. Embarrassment has personal and social value. That's the latest news from neuroscience via an ancestor who died in 1938.

# ECCLESIASTICUS 44:1-10, 13-14 132 B.C.

*Let us now sing the praises of our ancestors in their generations. God appointed to them great glory and majesty from the beginning.*
*There are those who ruled in their realms,*
*And made a name for themselves in their valor;*
*Those who gave counsel because they were intelligent;*
*Those who spoke prophetically, those who were wise in their instruction; those who composed musical tunes or put verse in writing, those living peacefully in their own homes –*
*All these were honored in their generation and were the pride of their times. Some of them left behind a name, so that others declare their praise.*

*But of others where is no memory;*
*They have perished as though they had never existed.*
*They have become as though they had never been born; but these also were godly, whose righteous deeds have not been forgotten.*
*Their offspring will continue forever and their glory will not be blotted out.*
*Their bodies are buried in peace...but they live on, generation after generation.*

The Wisdom of Jesus ben Sirach, a modern translation

# ACKNOWLEDGEMENTS

Writing a first work of historical fiction is a lot like rolling a boulder uphill. The writer needs help, especially when she is new to the art of composing family-based stories. I appreciate the many friends, colleagues and family members who put their shoulders to the boulder and helped move *The Edgefielders* upward. I offer grateful thanks to everyone - named and unnamed - who helped make this book happen.

Special thanks to Pete Nelson, whose loving presence, hearty whole-grain bread and tender touch gave me the strength to write on.

To Tim Hills and Sharon Nesbit for valuable insights into Edgefield's early years when its land and buildings served indigent citizens as the Multnomah County Poor Farm.

To Julie Steinbach for long walks, patient listening and inspired networking.

To John Brantingham at Mt. San Antonio College for producing the Writer's Conference that brought me into a circle of skillful teachers and enthusiastic companions.

To Ron Carlson whose early views on this particular boulder encouraged me to keep pushing.

To Judy Kohnen, Marta Chausee, Sue Buckwell, Betty Lane, Teri Tompkins, Patty Clark, Kevin Ridgeway, Sandra Walker and Charlotte Cousins for caring critiques and precise perspectives on character development.

To Lois and Ward McAfee for sheltering me so generously during extended writing retreats in Wrightwood.

To Jacqueline Chase, Judy Chatfield, Barbara Troxell, Jack Jackson, Rupert Nelson, Anna May Towne, Peg Wallace and Frances McConel for generous editorial judgments.

To Bruce McAllister for coaching me through the valley of the shadow of doubt with cheerful competence.

To Martha Alderson for introducing me to the brilliance of plot whispering.

To Ivan Doig for gracefully saying no.

To Frank Rogers, Charleen Krueger, Steve Smith and Jan Arkills for willing work, deep insights and impeccable judgment.

To Sigrid Wright for artistic editing, graphic design and faithful accompaniment.

To Carol Shields, Jeffrey Eugenides and Martha Southgate for modeling a form of writing I admire. Each has artfully composed narratives in which some characters speak occasionally while one serves as the primary voice. In future writings I aspire to interweave characters' voices the way these authors have done in *The Stone Diaries, Middlesex* and *The Taste of Salt*.

I accept full responsibility for the shortcomings of this book and appreciate each and every soul, living and dead, who assisted in creating it.

# QUESTIONS for REFLECTION and DISCUSSION

1. What do you know about the Great Depression? Public poor farms? Western Oregon's rain? How are era, place and weather central to the story?

2. How does Margaret Mary feel about herself before she meets Doctor Furst?

3. What changes do you see in her as a result of interactions with Lily White?

4. What was Lily up to when she dumped a tangle of yarn in the patient's lap?

5. How do the temperaments of doctors, nurses and physical therapist influence the way you feel about the infirmary? About Edgefield?

6. What does Lily White do to challenge Margaret Mary to volunteer in the infirmary?

7. Have you ever experienced a connection between your own healing and being of service to others?

8. Based on what you know about Margaret Mary and George how are they alike? How do they differ?

9. What helps Margaret Mary accept that it's over, that George has ended their long marriage?

10. Do you think it's harder for a woman to make peace with a deeply flawed mother or a deeply flawed husband? What leads you to this choice?

11. Why does Margaret Mary believe in the power of prayer? How did mystical experiences lead her to question her own sanity?

12. Why was Fudge an appropriate nickname for Mabel May?

13. How did candy nicknames contribute to building trust between strangers of different races?

14. In the first serious problem that Divinity and Fudge encountered, what was it about the women that enabled them to resolve their differences?

15. Margaret Mary's perspective colored this conflict with Mabel May. How might Peppermint Tillie have described it? How might Jasper have seen it?

16. Do you see any way in which Margaret Mary's relationship with Mabel May parallels her relationship with her own birth mother? With her Mother Superior at the convent?

17. What led Margaret Mary to toss out a lifeline to Cracker Jack?

18. Margaret Mary had ties to her home in North Portland and her birthplace in Hay, Ontario. Gradually she established ties to Edgefield. How do these three places become characters in the story?

19. How do you see Marigold as a healer? What was unusual about the feline's behavior in the infirmary?

QUESTIONS FOR REFLECTION AND DISCUSSION

20. What personal qualities did Doctor Furst demonstrate in the way he treated the cat?

21. What are Margaret Mary's unlikely qualifications for the role of hospice helper?

22. Why are unexpected rewards sometimes more valued than the ones we expect to receive?

23. George and Ben both struggled with alcoholism. Did Margaret Mary harbor attachments of her own?

24. What role did knitting play in her growth? In developing bonds between the women and the men?

25. Margaret Mary has conflicting feelings about both the family she came from and the family she created. How does this ambivalence affect her relationships at Edgefield?

26. If Margaret Mary had been able to make a life with Ben do you think the other Edgefielders would have supported or opposed their marriage? Why?

27. What motivated her to collaborate with Ben and Jasper in trying to foil the plot against Joshua?

28. How does the attack on Joshua influence the outlook and actions of the Edgefielders?

29. What impact do you think religion had on the inmates' common life at Edgefield? What are your feelings about this?

30. What role did music play in Margaret Mary's spiritual journey? Can you think of other songs she and her friends might have sung along the way?

31. Why do you think the author focused on her great-grandmother's experience in community rather than writing a personal memoir about Margaret Mary?

32. How is telling the truth different from writing the facts?

33. While residents and staff in many institutions are challenged by racial and religious differences, relatively few works of fiction describe the work of transformation within an intentional community. Why might this be so?

34. What was it about Edgefield that leads you to see it as a model public institution? Why or why not?

35. Do you sense any connection between Margaret Mary's encounter with Granny Brigid and her advice to "Welcome your embarrassment"?

36. Have you ever received a message from beyond the grave? Known anyone who did?

WHICH QUESTIONS WOULD YOU CHANGE?
WHAT QUESTIONS WOULD YOU ADD?

Tell the author at judithfavor@gmail.com

# LISTENING FOR THE SOUL

These days, many people seek healing and wholeness as Margaret Mary did in the Thirties. Some yearn for peace and well-being. Others are on a quest for meaning and purpose. Listening for the soul means helping one another connect with sources of Love. It means living as if each one of us is created in the image and likeness of God. Soul listening invites us to discern how to participate in Spirit's ongoing creative and redemptive work.

As inmates at Edgefield discovered, spiritual matters are best addressed together. Listening for the soul is not only the responsibility of pastors and doctors but also the privilege of friends and family. Soul care belongs within circles of trust, within communities of faith. Readers who are curious about ways to tend one's own soul while caring for the spiritual concerns of others can find guidance in many places. The author heartily recommends:

<u>A Hidden Wholeness: The Journey Toward an Undivided Life</u> by Parker Palmer, Jossey Bass, San Francisco, 2004.

<u>Spirituality for Extroverts (And Tips for Those Who Love Them)</u> by Nancy Reeves, Abingdon Press, Nashville, 2008.

<u>Listening for the Soul: Pastoral Care and Spiritual Direction</u> by Jean Stairs, Fortress Press, Minneapolis, 2000.

*God of Love: A Guide to the Heart of Judaism, Christinaity and Islam* by Mirabai Starr, Monkfish Publishing Company, Rhinebeck NY, 2012.

*An Altar in the World: A Geography of Faith* by Barbara Brown Taylor, HarperCollins, New York, 2009.

## ABOUT THE AUTHOR

Judith Wright Favor was born and raised in Portland, Oregon. She raised three children in Chico, California, served as a pastor in San Francisco and taught at Claremont School of Theology. She facilitates Spiritual Journey groups with Stillpoint in Southern California and at Ghost Ranch, New Mexico. She lives with her husband at Pilgrim Place in Claremont, California.

Judith wrote these tales to give voice to people who lost livelihoods and homes during the Great Depression. This is her first work of biographical fiction.

## ABOUT THE BOOK

*The Edgefielders: Poor House Tales of a Great-Grandmother* chronicles the Depression-era secrets and misadventures of a colorful crowd of paupers. Margaret Mary Wright lands at the Poor Farm in 1934 where she must make a home for herself among saints and sinners of all ages, races and religions.

This is a work of historical imagination, personal acceptance, unlikely romance and unexpected redemption.

## ORDER MORE COPIES

Contact your local bookstore or Amazon.com for additional copies of *The Edgefielders: Poor Farm Tales of a Great-Grandmother*. The author encourages group discussions that encourage listening for the soul.

Made in the USA
Charleston, SC
26 August 2013